THE
GREAT TRIBULATION

Rescuing Christians from Fear of the Future

Dr. Stanford E. Murrell

Ichthus Publications · Apollo, Pennsylvania

Copyright © 2019 by Stanford E. Murrell

This book was originally published by Wipf and Stock publishers under the title, *The Great Tribulation, A Historical Reality: A Biblical Alternative for Those Who have been Taught to Fear the Future*.

All rights reserved. No part of this publication may be reproduced, stored in a retrieval system, or transmitted, in any form or by any means, electronic, mechanical, photocopying, recording or otherwise, without prior permission of the publisher or the Copyright Licensing Agency.

Our goal is to provide high-quality, thought-provoking books that foster encouragement and spiritual growth. For more information regarding Ichthus Publications, other IP books, or bulk purchases, visit us online or write to support@ichthuspublications.com.

Unless otherwise indicated, all Scripture quotations are taken from the New King James Version®. Copyright © 1982 by Thomas Nelson. Used by permission. All rights reserved.

Cover image: Destruction of the Jerusalem Temple by Francesco Hayez

Printed in the United States of America

The Great Tribulation: Rescuing Christians from Fear of the Future
ISBN: 978-1-946971-58-6

www.ichthuspublications.com

"For these be days of Vengeance..."

—L u k e   2 1 : 2 2

For Mr. E. D. King of Rogers, Arkansas

Contents

1	A Terrible Picture	9
2	An Earnest Inquiry	19
3	Signs of the Times	37
4	After the Destruction of Jerusalem	71
5	The Sign of the Son of Man	75
6	Instruction from a Parable	83
7	An Important Doctrine	89

Appendix 1: Doctrine of the Coming of Christ   97

Appendix 2: The Greatest Prophecy Ever Fulfilled
A Study of Daniel 9:24–27   103

1

A Terrible Picture

A CALL FOR KINDNESS

In the conclusion to his important book, *The Great Tribulation*, William R. Kimball issues a call for Christian charity when discussing prophetic matters. The counsel of Mr. Kimball is worth keeping in mind.

> The highly speculative nature of prophetic interpretation, coupled with a myriad of conflicting viewpoints, presents Christianity with a potentially volatile area of disagreement and confrontation. This potential for disagreement and discord presents a serious challenge to every believer in striving to maintain the essential balance of peace with those who may earnestly disagree with us concerning our private prophetic positions. Our differences should never cause us to malign the sincerity or genuineness of those who

do not side with our opinions. Our essential unity and fellowship in Christ should never be severed or undermined because of our differences on prophetic points. Our eschatological differences should never be made a ground of fellowship, a test of orthodoxy, or a necessary element in Christian doctrine. We must faithfully exercise the spirit of liberty and charity towards opposing viewpoints. As the old maxim goes, "In essentials unity, in non-essentials liberty, in all things charity." If we must disagree with one another in defending our prophetic opinions—we must agree to disagree—agreeably. In the final analysis, our prophetic appraisals must always be tempered by that wisdom which is from above, which is pure, peaceable, gentle, easy to be entreated, full of mercy and good fruits, without partiality, and without hypocrisy (Jas. 3:17). In spite of whatever divergence of opinions we may possess concerning our private prophetic positions, may we all continue striving together in the faith of the gospel, looking for, hastening unto, and loving His appearing.[1]

A GOOD PLACE TO BEGIN

With an earnest desire to build up the body of Christ, with a deep conviction in the historic Christian ideals that the Word of God is the final authority for all matters of faith

---

[1] Kimball, *The Great Tribulation*, 260–61.

and practice, the biblical teaching concerning the great tribulation should be examined. A logical and proper place to commence the study is Matthew 24, Mark 13, and Luke 21. In these parallel Gospel accounts Jesus Christ sets forth specific events that would happen within a fixed historical period. A critical passage for establishing the people and the place of the great tribulation period is Matthew 24:34. After speaking of false Christs, wars and rumors of wars, after teaching about the abomination of desolation spoken of by Daniel the prophet, after warning of a great tribulation unseen since the beginning of the world, Jesus told His disciples something amazing by saying: "Verily, I say unto you, this generation shall not pass, till all these things be fulfilled" (Matthew 24:34). When accepted in a normal, literal, grammatical, historical context it becomes very plain that Jesus was telling about prophetic events that would be fulfilled within the very life-time of those who were listening to Him speak. The evidence for this is confirmed by letting biblical Scripture interpret Scripture.

"THIS GENERATION"

The following passages should be studied to find out how the phrase "this generation" is used throughout the Scriptures.

- "But to what shall I liken *this generation?*" (Matthew 11:16).

- "The men of Nineveh will rise up in the judgment with *this generation* and condemn it . . ." (Matthew 12:41).
- "The queen of the South will rise up in the judgment with *this generation* and condemn it" (Matthew 12:42).
- ". . . So shall it also be with *this wicked generation*" (Matthew 12:45).
- "Assuredly, I say to you, all these things will come upon *this generation*" (Matthew 23:36).
- "Assuredly, I say to you, *this generation* will by no means pass away till all these things take place" (Matthew 23:34).
- "For whoever is ashamed of Me and My words in *this adulterous and sinful generation*" (Mark 8:38).
- "Assuredly, I say to you, *this generation* will by no means pass away till all these things take place" (Mark 13:30).
- "And while the crowds were thickly gathered together, He began to say, '*This is an evil generation. It seeks a sign, and no sign will be given to it except the sign of Jonah the prophet*'" (Luke 11:29).
- "For as Jonah became a sign to the Ninevites, so also the Son of Man will be to *this generation*" (Luke 11:30).
- "The queen of the South will rise up in the judgment with the men of *this generation* and condemn them," (Luke 11:31).

- "The men of Nineveh will rise up in the judgment with *this generation* and condemn it" (Luke 11:32).
- "from the blood of Abel to the blood of Zechariah who perished between the altar and the temple. Yes, I say to you, it shall be required of *this generation*" (Luke 11:51).
- "But first He must suffer many things and be rejected by *this generation*" (Luke 17:25).
- "Assuredly, I say to you, *this generation* will by no means pass away till all things take place" (Luke 21:32).
- "And with many other words he testified and exhorted them, saying, 'Be saved from *this perverse generation*'" (Acts 2:40).

When the Word of God wants to indicate a different generation from that of the present one being addressed, the proper language is used. One such example is found in Hebrews 3:10 where the Lord says He was grieved with "that generation." Everyone understands the generation with which the Lord was not pleased was the Exodus generation, which had come out of Egypt under the leadership of Moses. That much is evident from the preceding words, verses 8–9 of Hebrews 3. To contend that in Matthew 24, Mark 13, and Luke 21, Jesus was speaking of events yet to come in a future, distant generation is confusing at best and a violation of the normal usage of language. Jesus spoke prophetically of many events that would come to pass in the generation in which the disciples lived. History confirms that what the Lord said would happen did happen. Consider the following.

THE STORY BEGINS

Between A.D. 66 and A.D. 70, the prophetic utterances of Jesus in Matthew 24, Mark 13, and Luke 21 began to be fulfilled. Briefly the known facts can be stated. In the summer of the year A.D. 66, a Jewish revolt broke out in Jerusalem. Led by fanatical zealots this revolt took place against the overbearing Roman procurator of Judea named Gessius Florus because he had allowed a massacre of Jews in Caesarea. From May through November the Jews reacted against his oppressive reign. As a result, Neapolitanus, a Roman military tribune, was sent from Antioch by Cestius Gallus, the Roman governor of Syria, to try to calm the Jews. The Jews refused to be pacified and in the battle that followed they were able to repress the troops of the governor of Syria. Cestius had to order a retreat, much to the delight of the Jews. During his withdrawal to the coast his army was assaulted near Beth Horon. Cestius Gallus was able to escape but many men and much military material was left behind. He died in the spring of A.D. 67 with the stigma of his forces having suffered the worst Roman defeat by Jewish rebels.

When word finally reached the emperor Nero in Rome about the explosive situation unfolding in Israel, Nero commissioned a seasoned general, Vespasian, to put down the revolt against imperial Rome and to restore the *Pax Romana* (the Roman peace). War against the Jews in

A TERRIBLE PICTURE

Jerusalem was officially declared in February, A.D. 67, when Vespasian received his commission from Nero.

In the Spring of A.D. 67, Vespasian finally arrived to take charge of the operations in Jerusalem. But the Jews proved to be a strong and resourceful people, not easily subdued. They desperately wanted to be free of Roman bondage and were willing to die in the fight for freedom. History records that Jerusalem did finally fall to Titus, the son of Vespasian, who took charge of the siege in the late summer of A.D. 70 because his father had to return to Rome in July of A.D. 69 to rule the empire following the suicidal death of the madman Nero. For about forty-two months the Jewish people held out against the greatest military power on the face of the earth. And then Jerusalem fell.

In broad strokes this was the terrible picture of death and destruction, violence and chaos between A.D. 66 and A.D. 70. The words of Jesus in Matthew 24, Mark 13, and Luke 21 can be used to supply some of the gory details of this period. What will emerge is a historical fulfillment of the great tribulation that Jesus predicted would come upon the generation He ministered to. These were days of vengeance as God poured out His wrath on those who dared to kill His Son. The evidence is compelling for a historical fulfillment of the Lord's prophetic utterances of a great tribulation upon Israel culminating in A.D. 70. Those who were eyewitnesses of the events testify to the judgment of God upon the land. One of the leading eyewitnesses for the history of this time period was a man called Josephus. A number of facts are known about Josephus.

JOSEPHUS: EYEWITNESS TO HISTORY

Flavius Josephus was born in either A.D. 37 or A.D. 38. He was named Joseph ben Matthias (Joseph, son of Matthias). Since he was born into a priestly family, Josephus was educated in both Jewish and Hellenistic cultures. Intellectually gifted, Josephus was a child prodigy and at the age of fourteen was consulted by the chief priests and community leaders concerning the meaning of the Jewish ordinances. At the age of sixteen, Josephus began to investigate the major Jewish sects with the intent to join the one that demonstrated the most piety. At the age of nineteen he joined the Pharisees.

Josephus quietly performed his religious duties until he was twenty-six years old when he was catapulted into national prominence. It happened this way. Felix the Procurator of Judea (A.D. 52–60) who sat in judgment on the apostle Paul, imprisoned several priests and sent them to Rome on a minor charge. Josephus was sent to Rome to try to obtain their release. On his journey, Josephus was shipwrecked but was rescued and continued on his journey. Once in Rome, Josephus managed to befriend Alityrus, a Jewish actor who was a favorite of Nero. Through this connection Josephus was able to obtain the release of the priests. Returning to Palestine, Josephus found many of his fellow Jews preparing for a revolt against Rome. He argued against such action, then bowed to the social and political pressures of nationalism and joined the rebellion.

At the age of thirty, while in Galilee on a mission from the leadership in Jerusalem, Josephus witnessed the advance of the army of Vespasian in the spring of A.D. 67. He took refuge in the fortress at Jotapata. Forty-seven days later the fortress fell and Josephus was taken as a prisoner of war to Vespasian. In the presence of the important Roman general, Josephus uttered the unlikely prediction that Vespasian would soon be the Emperor of Rome. The general was impressed. In July, A.D. 69, Vespasian was indeed proclaimed Emperor of Rome by his own soldiers.

Unfortunately for him, the relationships that Josephus cultivated with the Romans made him *persona non grata* among many of his own people. The capable diplomat had other problems, especially at home, for Josephus was married three times. The first wife was a captive woman from Caesarea. The second wife was from Alexandria. By this wife Josephus had three children but only one, Hyrcanes, survived. The third wife was a Jewish woman from Crete who became the mother of Justus and Agrippa. Josephus died in the year A.D. 100 but not before recording several large historical narratives. His major works are: *The Jewish War, Antiquities of the Jews, The Life,* and *Against Apion.*

As a writer of events, Josephus is considered to be a reliable historian. It is noteworthy that it was the Christian community that preserved the works of Josephus and not the Jewish community which considered him to be a traitor. The works of Josephus were preserved by the early Christians because he made reference to Jesus Christ. Josephus also recorded those events the early church came to believe were the fulfilled prophecy of Christ in Matthew 24, Mark 13, and Luke 21.

2

An Earnest Inquiry

SPECIFIC QUESTIONS

Turning to the Gospel narratives, the initial words of Jesus are given as He responded to specific questions raised by His disciples. The biblical narrative is very clear. Jesus and His disciples were in the temple of Jerusalem. The disciples were very impressed with the magnificent structure. They pointed to the building and said unto the Lord: "...Teacher, see what manner of stones and what buildings *are here!*" (Mark 13:1).

The Temple was indeed magnificent, not only for its architectural beauty, but also for its rich historical setting that can be traced back to Abraham. From the moment Abraham was willing to sacrifice his only son to God on the site of Mount Moriah (2 Chronicles 3:1; also called Mount Zion) the place has been a sacred spot to the nation of Israel.

Here the Temple was built. Here the Temple was rebuilt after being destroyed in 586 B.C. by the Babylonians.

Two basic Temples have stood on Mount Zion: the Temple which Solomon built and the reconstructed Temple of Zerubbabel following the seventy years of captivity in Babylon. The reconstructed Temple was dedicated in 515 B.C. For those who remembered the beauty, size, and opulence of Solomon's Temple, the reconstructed Temple paled in comparison (Haggai 2:3).

Time passed and the Second Temple stood unchanged until the days of Christ under the reign of Herod the Great. Herod had no real interest in religion but he did enjoy engaging in extensive building programs. One of his many projects included the renovation of the Temple in Jerusalem that had been rebuilt by the returned exiles five hundred years before. In 19 B.C. the craftsmen of Herod began working on the Second Temple. In A.D. 64 the renovation was completed—just six years before the Temple was again destroyed, this time by the Romans.

A THIRD TEMPLE?

Since A.D. 70, many Jews have longed for a rebuilding of the Temple. Some people in the Christian community encourage such a construction. The concept and prophetic expectations for a third Jewish Temple to be rebuilt in Jerusalem is being promoted. Recent publications advocate a third Temple and prophetic speakers are strongly suggesting that all is ready for the Temple to be constructed. Militant zealots speak of how easy it would be with modern weapons to destroy the great Mosque of El Aksah that has occupied the site of Solomon's Temple area for 1000 years. There is talk of secret plans for the construction of a third Temple. In 2001, a symbolic cornerstone was cut and dedicated at the Dung Gate, the southern entrance to the Jewish quarter of the walled Old City. While the hopes and dreams of a third Temple remains, while speculation continues, it is often forgotten that God has already spoken on this whole matter.

THE NEED TO REFOCUS

It should be remembered there was a Temple that once existed and which saw the establishment of all God's promises and purposes in Christ realized. The Temple was the Second Temple rebuilt under the leadership of Ezra, Nehemiah, and Zerrubbabel following the Babylonian captivity of 606–538 B.C. The first Temple, or Solomon's Temple, was destroyed in 586 B.C. The Jews built the Second Temple after they returned from the Captivity. The Second Temple was not as impressive as the one originally built by Solomon and yet the prophets arose to tell the people the Lord would honor the Second Temple by sending the Messiah to it. Here are the wonderful words of Haggai with the Divine promise:

> Thus saith the LORD of hosts: Yet once, it is a little while, and I will shake the heavens and the earth and the sea and the dry land; And I will shake all nations and the Desire of

> all Nations shall come, and I will fill this house with the glory, saith the LORD of hosts. The silver is mine, and the gold is mine, saith the LORD of hosts. The glory of this latter house shall be greater than the former [i.e. Solomon's Temple] saith the LORD of Hosts, and in this place will I give peace, saith the LORD of Hosts (Hag. 2:6–9).

Haggai was speaking at the dedication of the Second Temple built by Ezra and others who returned from the great captivity. He was declaring that despite the more inferior structure the Second Temple would still be honored and it was, for the Lord Jesus did come to this very Temple.

With the coming of the Messiah, heaven and earth shook. The shaking of heaven and earth denotes the passing of the Old Covenant and the establishment of the New Covenant. On the day of Pentecost, Peter quoted a similar prophecy from Joel to establish this eschatological event.

> I will show wonders in heaven above And signs in the earth beneath: Blood and fire and vapor of smoke. The sun shall be turned into darkness, And the moon into blood, Before the coming of the great and awesome day of the LORD. And it shall come to pass *That* whoever calls on the name of the LORD Shall be saved. (Acts 2:19–21).

There are some very serious theological problems for the conservative Christian if the Temple vision of Ezekiel were to be considered to be a prophetic reference to a third Temple that is literal and is to be built in the future. The following points should be considered.

EZEKIEL'S TEMPLE VISION

First, the construction of a third temple would challenge Christ's current eternal priesthood for then the sons of Zadok would have the last exalted position over Melchizedek and Aaron's priesthood (Ezek. 44:15–16, 23). Of the Messiah, "The LORD has sworn And will not relent, 'You *are* a priest forever According to the order of Melchizedek.'" (Ps. 110:4). The author of Hebrews argues that Jesus is made a "surety of a better testament" (Heb. 7:21) and "has an unchangeable priesthood" (Heb. 7:24). A return to a carnal priesthood supervised by the sons of Zadok would invalidate the priestly superiority of Jesus.

Second, the construction of a third temple would reintroduce sin offerings made by the blood of bulls and goats. It has been suggested the sacrifices of a future third temple during the millennium period would be for a memorial, but many times in Ezekiel the sin offering is mentioned without qualification (Ezek. 43:19, 21, 25, etc.) The word "memorial" is used twenty-nine times in the Old Testament and three times in the New Testament. The term is not used in the book of Ezekiel. The faithful commentator will exegete the Scriptures and does not engage in eisegesis, that is to say, reading into the text private opinions.

Third, the entire purpose of Ezekiel's vision is lost if it be literal. The Lord spoke to Ezekiel and told him the very object or purpose of the vision was to show the perfect holiness of the Lord by which the people of Israel might measure the extent of their iniquities and repent.

> "Son of man, describe the temple to the house of Israel, that they may be ashamed of their iniquities; and let them measure the pattern. And if they are ashamed of all that they have done, make known to them the design of the temple and its arrangement, its exits and its entrances, its entire design and all its ordinances, all its forms and all its laws. Write *it* down in their sight, so that they may keep its whole design and all its ordinances, and perform them. This *is* the law of the temple: The whole area surrounding the mountaintop *is* most holy. Behold, this *is* the law of the temple (Ezek. 43:10–12).

Fourth, if Ezekiel's vision temple is to be interpreted literally, and remains a future event, then circumcision must be re-established as a requirement of access to God (Ezek. 44:9): "Thus says the LORD God; No foreigner [i.e., Gentile], uncircumcised in heart or uncircumcised in flesh, shall enter into My sanctuary, including any foreigner who *is* among the children of Israel." Long ago the apostle Paul found it necessary to withstand Peter face to face over the very issue of compelling early Christian converts to engage in the practice of circumcision (Gal. 2:11–16). So upset was Paul over this issue that he wrote to the Galatian believers with exasperation and righteous indignation, instructing them,

"And I, brethren, if I still preach circumcision, why do I still suffer persecution? Then the offense of the cross has ceased. I could wish that those who trouble you would even cut themselves off! [Greek, *apokopto*, castrated] (Gal. 5:11–12). Now, once again, in a very subtle, yet real, way the concept of mandatory circumcision for the people of God is unwisely being embraced within the body of Christ.

Fifth, if Ezekiel's vision temple is literal and futuristic, then the Lord will again come to dwell in a building. "Also He brought me by way of the north gate to the front of the temple; so I looked, and behold, the glory of the LORD filled the house of the LORD; and I fell on my face" (Ezek. 44:4). However, the New Testament unequivocally teaches the Lord *does not* dwell in temples made with hands, neither is there an expectation that He will. "However, the Most High does not dwell in temples made with hands, as the prophet says" (Acts 7:48).

Sixth, if Ezekiel's vision temple is to be understood literally and in a future context then there will once again be priests of a Levitical order who will be required to avoid woolen undergarments lest they sweat. "They shall have linen bonnets upon their heads, and shall have linen breeches upon their loins; they shall not gird themselves with any thing that causeth sweat" (Ezek. 44:18 KJV). These future priests must also abide by other stringent personal care such as cutting their hair to a prescribed length (Ezek. 44:20), avoiding contact with the dead (Ezek. 44:31), and receiving the first of the sacrificial flour in order to bestow a priestly blessing (Ezek. 44:3). Yet, the New Testament stands in opposition to implementing the Old Testament ceremonial practices for the church. The entire book of Hebrews is an apologetic against the Christian community returning to the Levitical priesthood—*because there is a better way.*

Seventh, if Ezekiel's vision temple is to be understood to be literal and yet future, there will be again on earth, following the Second Advent and with the Lord's approval, all that Christ came to abolish: sin, suffering, ritual bloody sacrifices, and death.

Eighth, in Ezekiel 47, the highlight of the temple vision is found in the living waters rising inside the Temple and issuing from the threshold. The river flows from the Temple, getting deeper and wider in its course as it sweeps across the country till it empties itself into the Dead Sea where it heals the waters. Everything springs to life where the water flows. Fishermen stand upon the banks of the river and fill their baskets and spread their nets. Trees of paradise flourish on either bank yielding a continuous harvest of fruit and yielding their leaves as healing medicine. Spiritually, this is a lovely and wonderful description of the gospel river of grace flowing from Jerusalem until it comes to cover the earth with the knowledge of the glory of the Lord as the waters cover the seas (Isa. 11:9, John 2:21 cf. John 7:37–38).

Finally, Hebrews 9:1–14 teaches the tabernacle and, of necessity, therefore, the temple are only a type of heavenly things and figures of the true. The shadow must give way to the substance. All rituals must vanish as the reality of the work of Christ at Calvary rises to have preeminence. "For Christ has not entered the holy places made with hands, *which are* copies of the true, but into heaven itself, now to appear in the presence of God for us" (Heb. 9:24).

> Come, ye sinners, poor and needy,
>   Weak and wounded, sick and sore;
> Jesus ready stands to save you,
>   Full of pity, joined with power:
> He is able, He is able,
>   He is willing: doubt no more.
>
> Come, ye weary, heavy-laden,
>   Bruised and mangled by the Fall;
> If you tarry till you're better,
>   You will never come at all;
> Not the righteous, not the righteous-
>   Sinners Jesus came to call.
>
> Let not conscience make you linger,
>   Nor of fitness fondly dream;
> All the fitness He requireth
>   Is to feel your need of Him:
> This He gives you, this He gives you;
>   'Tis the Spirit's rising beam.[2]

There is no need for a literal third temple to teach anyone anything, for spiritual reality has come in the Person of Jesus Christ. There is no need for a literal third temple to fulfill any prophetic utterances, for all which the prophets spoke about has been fulfilled in the Lord. "And beginning

---

[2] Joseph Hart.

at Moses and all the prophets, he [Jesus] expounded unto them [the two disciples on the road to Emmaus] in all the scriptures the things concerning himself" (Luke 24:27 KJV). In light of these Gospel truths there is no need for the Christian community to anticipate, desire, or promote the rebuilding of a third Jewish temple. If such a temple is ever rebuilt in the course of human history, it will not be based upon any biblical mandate.

DESTRUCTION OF THE SECOND TEMPLE

Despite His disciples being impressed with the buildings that constituted the Second Temple, Jesus was not. The Lord began to tell them what would happen to that which so many loved more than the Messiah. The words of Jesus are vivid and precise. "And Jesus said to them, 'Do you not see all these things? Assuredly, I say to you, not *one* stone shall be left here upon another, that shall not be thrown down'" (Matt. 24:2). Mark records it this way: "And Jesus answered and said to him, 'Do you see these great buildings? Not *one* stone shall be left upon another, that shall not be thrown down'" (Mark 13:2). Luke says: "These things which you see—the days will come in which not *one* stone shall be left upon another that shall not be thrown down" (Luke 21:6). History records that the holy Temple, just as Jesus foretold, was utterly destroyed. Josephus records the terrible scene.

The Temple is Burned

Writing in his multi-volume, *The War of the Jews*, the ancient historian Josephus records the gruesome scene:

> So Titus retired into the tower of Antonia, and resolved to storm the temple the next day, early in the morning, with his whole army, and encamp round about the holy house; but, as for the house, God had for certain long ago doomed it to the fire; and now that fatal day was come, according to the revolution of ages: it was the tenth day of the month Lous (Ab), upon which it was formerly burnt by the king of Babylon; although these flames took their rise from the Jews themselves, and were occasioned by them; for upon Titus's retiring, the seditious lay still for a little while, and then attacked the Romans again, when those that guarded the holy house fought with those that quenched the fire that was burning in the inner (court of the) temple; but these Romans put the Jews to flight, and proceeded as far as the holy house itself. At which time one of the soldiers, without staying for any orders, and without any concern or dread upon him at so great an undertaking, and being hurried on by a certain divine fury, snatched somewhat out of the materials that were on fire, and being lifted up by another soldier, he set fire to a golden window, through which there was a passage to the rooms that were round about the holy house, on the

north side of it. As the flames went upward the Jews made a great clamor, such as so mighty an affliction required, and ran together to prevent it; and now they spared not their lives any longer, nor suffered anything to restrain their force, since that holy house was perishing, for whose sake it was that they kept such a guard about it.

And now a certain person came running to Titus, and told him of this fire, as he was resting himself in his tent after the last battle; whereupon he rose up in great haste and, as he was, ran to the holy house, in order to have a stop put to the fire; after him followed all his commanders, and after them followed the several legions, in great astonishment; so there was great clamor and tumult raised, as was natural upon the disorderly motion of so great an army.

Then did Caesar, both by calling to the soldiers that were fighting, with a loud voice, and by giving a signal to them with his right hand, ordered them to quench the fire; but they did not hear what he said, though he spake so loud, having their ears already dimmed by the greater noise another way; nor did they attend to the signal he made with his hand neither, as still some of them were distracted with fighting, and others with passion; but as for the legions that came running thither, neither any persuasions nor any threatenings could restrain their violence, but each one's own passion was his commander at this time; and as they were crowding into the temple together, many of them were trampled on by one another, while a great number fell among the ruins of the cloisters, which were still hot and smoking, and were destroyed in the same miserable way with those whom they had conquered: and when they were come near the holy house, they made as if they did not so much as hear Caesar's orders to the contrary; but they encouraged those that were before them to set it on fire.

As for the seditious, they were in too great distress already to afford their assistance (towards quenching the fire); they were everywhere slain, and everywhere beaten; as for a great part of the people, they were weak and without arms, and had their throats cut wherever they were caught. Now, round about the altar lay dead bodies heaped one upon another; as at the steps going up to it ran a great quantity of their blood, wither also the dead bodies that were slain above (on the altar) fell down. And now, since Caesar was no way able to restrain the enthusiastic fury of the soldiers, and the fire proceeded on more and more, he went into the holy place of the temple, with his commanders, and saw it, with what was in it, which he found to be far superior to what the relations of foreigners contained, and not inferior to what we ourselves boasted of and believed about it; but as the flame had not as yet reached to its inward parts, but was still consuming the rooms that were about the holy house, and Titus supposing what the fact was, that the house itself might yet be saved, he came in haste and endeavored to persuade the soldiers to quench the fire, and gave order to Liberality the centurion, and one of those spearmen that were about him, to beat the soldiers that were refractory with their staves, and to restrain them; yet were their passions too hard for the regards they had for Caesar, and the dread they had of him who forbade them, as was their hatred of the Jews, and a certain vehement inclination to fight them, too hard for them also.

Moreover, the hope of plunder induced many to go on, as having this opinion, that all the places within were full of money, and as seeing that all round about it was made of gold; and besides, one of those that went into the place prevented Caesar, when he ran so hastily out to restrain the soldiers, and threw the fire upon the hinges of the gate, in the dark; whereby the flame burst out from within the holy house itself immediately, when the commanders retired, and Caesar with them, and when nobody any longer forbade those that were without to set fire to it; and thus was the holy house burnt down, without Caesar's approbation.[3]

---

[3] Josephus, *The War of the Jews*, Book 6, Chapter 4:5–7.

Jerusalem Under the Ban

Josephus describes the scene,

> While the holy house was on fire, everything was plundered that came to hand, and ten thousand of those that were caught were slain; nor was there a commiseration of any age, or any reverence of gravity; but children and old men, and profane persons, and priests, were all slain in the same manner; so that this war went round all sorts of men, and brought them to destruction, and as well those that made supplication for their lives as those that defended themselves by fighting. The flame was also carried a long way, and made an echo, together with the groans of those that were slain; and because this hill was high, and the works at the temple were very great, one would have thought the whole city had been on fire. Nor can one imagine anything either greater or more terrible than this noise, for there was at once a shout of the Roman legions, who were marching all together, and a sad clamor of the seditious, who were now surrounded with fire and sword.
>
> The people also that were left above were beaten back upon the enemy, and under a great consternation, and made sad moans at the calamity they were under; the multitudes also that was in the city joined in this outcry with those that were upon the hill; and besides, many of those that

were worn away by the famine, and their mouths almost closed, when they saw the fire of the holy house, they exerted their utmost strength, and brake out into groans and outcries again: Perea did also return the echo, as well as the mountains round about (the city), and augmented the force of the entire noise. Yet was the misery itself more terrible than this disorder; for one would have thought that the hill itself, on which the temple stood, was seething-hot, as full of fire, and those that were slain more in number than those that slew them; for the ground did nowhere appear visible, for the dead bodies that lay on it; but the soldiers went over heaps of these bodies, as they ran upon such as fled from them.

And now it was that the multitude of the robbers were thrust out (of the inner court of the temple) by the Romans, and had much ado to get into the outer court, and from thence into the city, while the remainder of the populace fled into the cloister of that outer court. As for the priests, some of them plucked up from the holy house the spikes that were upon it, with their bases, which were made of lead, and shot them at the Romans instead of darts.

But then as they gained nothing by so doing, and as the fire burst out upon them, they retired to the wall that was eight cubits broad, and there they tarried; yet did two of these of eminence among them, who might have saved themselves by going over to the Romans, or have borne up with courage, and taken their fortune with the others, threw themselves into the fire, and were burnt together with the holy house; their names were Meirus the son of Belgas, and Joseph the son of Daleus.[4]

PROPHECY FULFILLED

In A.D. 30, when Jesus spoke of the destruction of the Temple, the disciples could not fully appreciate what the Lord knew was going to happen. They could not envision the bloodshed and violence, the fire and destruction that was to come. However, when Jesus spoke in A.D. 30, the disciples were curious enough and alarmed enough to ask Him for more details.

> Now as He sat on the Mount of Olives, the disciples came to Him privately, saying, "Tell us, when will these things be? And what *will be* the sign of Your coming, and of the end of the age?" (Matt. 24:3).

> "Tell us, when will these things be? And what *will be* the sign when all these things will be fulfilled?" (Mark 13:4).

> So they asked Him, saying, "Teacher, but when will these things be? And what sign *will there*

---

[4] Josephus, *Wars*, Book 6, Chapter 5:1.

be when these things are about to take place?" (Luke 21:7).

3

Signs of the Times

TWO QUESTIONS

Two basic questions are asked based on Matthew 24:3, Mark 13:4, and Luke 21:7. First, "When shall the Temple be destroyed"? Second, "What sign shall there be when these things come to pass?"

THE FIRST SIGN

While the disciples asked for a single sign for the Second Coming and the end of the age, in grace the Lord gave them several signs that would characterize the period between A.D. 30 and the destruction of Jerusalem. He also gave them the specific sign they were looking for because the *"age"* (Greek, *aion,* not *kosmos* [world], as translated in Matthew 24:3) was indeed coming to an end. Out of Judaism God intended to bring the New Testament expression of the church just as He brought His chosen people out of Egypt long ago.

The first sign that Jesus gave to characterize the specific period in question (A.D. 30 – A.D. 70) was the rise of false Christs and deceivers. "And Jesus answered and said to them: 'Take heed that no one deceives you. For many will come in My name, saying, "I am the Christ,"' and will deceive many" (Matt. 24:4–5). The Gospel of Mark says, "And Jesus, answering them, began to say: 'Take heed that no one deceives you. For many will come in My name, saying, "I am *He*," and will deceive many'" (Mark 13:5–6). And Luke's account reads, "And He said: 'Take heed that you not be deceived. For many will come in My name, saying, "I am *He*," and, "The time has drawn near." Therefore do not go after them'" (Luke 21:8).

False Christs and Deceivers

The Jewish historian Josephus writes that many pretenders arose claiming Divine inspiration, claiming to be the promised Messiah. These men deceived the Jews by declaring that God would show the miraculous signs of deliverance from the Roman armies. Many people followed the false prophets into the desert.

> But there was an Egyptian false prophet that did the Jews more mischief than the former; for he was a cheat, and pretended to be a prophet also, and got together thirty thousand men that were deluded by him; these he led round about from the

wilderness to the mount which was called the Mount of Olives, and was ready to break into Jerusalem by force from that place; and if he could but once conquer the Roman garrison and the people, he intended to domineer over them by the assistance of those guards of his that were to break into the city with him, but Felix prevented his attempt, and met him with his Roman soldiers, while all the people assisted him in his attack upon them, insomuch that when it came to a battle, the Egyptian ran away, with a few others, while the greatest part of those that were with him were either destroyed or taken alive, but the rest of the multitude were dispersed every one to their own homes and there concealed themselves.[5]

During the reign of Nero, while Felix was procurator of Judea (Acts 23:26), deceivers and false prophets emerged to encourage the most immoral of behavior.

But for the marriage of Drusilla with Azizus, it was in no long time afterward dissolved, upon the following occasion:—While Felix was procurator of Judea, he saw this Drusilla, and fell in love with her; for she did indeed exceed all other women in beauty, and he sent to her a person whose name was Simon, one of his friends; a Jew he was, and by birth a Cypriot, and one who pretended to be a magician; and endeavored to persuade her to

---

[5] Josephus, *Wars*, Book 2, Chapter 13.

forsake her present husband, and marry him; and promised, that if she would not refuse him, he would make her a happy woman. Accordingly she acted ill, and because she was desirous to avoid her sister Bernice's envy, for she was very ill treated by her on account of her beauty, was prevailed upon to transgress the laws of her forefathers, and to marry Felix; and when he had a son by her, he named him Agrippa.

More Deceivers

The testimony to the rise of false Christ's and deceivers is also recorded in the book of Acts. Simon Magus is spoken of in Acts 8:9–10. The early Christian theologian and historian Jerome (c. A.D. 347–420) quotes Simon Magus as claiming, "I am the word of God, I am the comforter, I am almighty, I am all there is of God." Acts 5 records the work of Theudas (Acts 5:37) and in Acts 13 Paul confronted the false prophet Bar-Jesus. In secular history, Origen (c. A.D. 184–253) mentions a deceiver by the name of Dositheus who asserted that he was the Messiah spoken of by Moses. Then, there was Barchochebas who is supposed to have spit out flames. One of the more fanatical of the false Messiahs was the individual who appeared in A.D. 63. Historian Philip Schaff records the man and his message.

> Not long before the outbreak of the Jewish war, seven years before the siege of Jerusalem (A.D. 63), a peasant by the name of Joshua, or Jesus,

appeared in the city at the Feast of Tabernacles, and in a tone of prophetic ecstasy cried day and night on the street among the people: "A voice from the morning, a voice from the evening! A voice from the four winds! A voice of rain against Jerusalem and the Temple! A voice against the bridegrooms and the brides! A voice against the whole people! Woe, woe to Jerusalem!" The magistrates, terrified by this woe, had the prophet of evil taken up and scourged. He offered no resistance, and continued to cry his "Woe." Being brought before the procurator, Albinus, he was scourged till his bones could be seen, but interposed not a word for himself, uttered no curse on his enemies; simply exclaimed at every blow in a mournful tone: "Woe, woe to Jerusalem!" To the governor's question, who and whence he was, he answered nothing. Finally, they let him go, as a madman. But he continued for seven years and five months, till the outbreak of the war, especially at the three great feasts, to proclaim the approaching fall of Jerusalem. During the siege he was singing his dirge, for the last time, from the wall. Suddenly he added: "Woe, woe also to me!" and a stone of the Romans hurled at his head put an end to his prophetic lamentations.[6]

---

[6] Schaff, *History of the Christian Church*, Vol. 1, 393.

Wars and Rumors of Wars

Besides deceivers, Jesus also warned of wars and rumors of wars. "And you will hear of wars and rumors of wars. See that you are not troubled; for all *these things* must come to pass, but the end is not yet. For nation will rise against nation, and kingdom against kingdom. And there will be famines, pestilences, and earthquakes in various places" (Matt. 24:6–7). The Marcan Gospel reads, "But when you hear of wars and rumors of wars, do not be troubled; for *such things* must happen, but the end *is* not yet. For nation will rise against nation, and kingdom against kingdom. And there will be earthquakes in various places, and there will be famines and troubles. These *are* the beginnings of sorrows" (Mark 13:7–8). Finally, Luke's accounts reads, "'But when you hear of wars and commotions, do not be terrified; for these things must come to pass first, but the end *will* not *come* immediately.' Then He said to them, 'Nation will rise against nation, and kingdom against kingdom'" (Luke 21:9–10).

The forty-year period between the Olivet Discourse and the Fall of Jerusalem in A.D. 70 was turbulent, violent, and bloody. The Jews knew the horrors of civil war as well as their long-standing attempts at revolting against Rome. Scores of thousands of people perished in senseless agony. At Caesarea alone, 20,000 Jews were killed. At Scythopolis, 13,000 Jews were slaughtered. In Alexandria, 50,000 Jews were slain. In Damascus, another 10,000 Jews were killed. There were rumors of war when the increasingly cruel and insane emperor Caligula (A.D. 12 – A.D. 41) ordered his statue to be erected in the Temple of Jerusalem in A.D. 40. When the Jews refused, Rome threatened to march.

> Now Caius Caesar did so grossly abuse the fortune he had arrived at, as to take himself to be a god, and to desire to be so called also, and to cut off those of the greatest nobility out of his country. He also extended his impiety as far as the Jews. Accordingly, he sent Petronius with an army to Jerusalem, to place his statue in the temple, and commanded him that, in case the Jews would not admit of them, he should slay those that opposed it, and carry all the rest of the nation into captivity; but God concerned himself with these his commands. However, Petronius marched out of Antioch into Judea, with three legions, and many Syrian auxiliaries. Now as to the Jews, some of them could not believe the stories that spoke of a war; but those that did believe them were in the utmost distress how to defend themselves, and the terror diffused itself presently through them all, for the army was already come to Ptolemais.[7]

Just as Jesus predicted, there were wars and rumors of wars during this time of A.D. 30 through A.D. 70.

---

[7] Josephus, Wars, Book 2, Chapter 10:1.

Famines, Pestilence, and Earthquakes

Continuing the narrative, Jesus foretold there would be famines, pestilence, and earthquakes. "For nation will rise against nation, and kingdom against kingdom. And there will be famines, pestilences, and earthquakes in various places" (Matt. 24:7). Mark reads, "For nation will rise against nation, and kingdom against kingdom. And there will be earthquakes in various places, and there will be famines and troubles. These *are* the beginnings of sorrows" (Mark 13:8). Luke adds, "And there will be great earthquakes in various places, and famines and pestilences; and there will be fearful sights and great signs from heaven" (Luke 21:11).

The book of Acts records the outbreak of famines in the days of Claudius Caesar (A.D. 44) in Acts 11:28. The saints at Antioch were moved to send relief to Judean Christians. Still, many died. Besides the famine in Judea, there were other famines that appeared during the reign of Claudius. One was located in Greece and two in Rome as recorded by the Roman consul and noted historian Dio Cassius (c. A.D. 150–235) and Tacitus (A.D. 56–117), a senator and historian of the Roman Empire. During that period, another reputable historian, Suetonius (c. A.D. 69–c. 122), also records famines devastated the region. During the reign of Nero (A.D. 54–68), in one year, 30,000 people died of starvation though he had made efforts to build up stocks against winter-time famine.

During the reign of Claudius (A.D. 41–54), earthquakes occurred in Crete, Smyrna, Miletus, Chios and Samos. Tacitus mentioned earthquakes at Rome, writing that frequent earthquakes occurred, by which many houses were thrown down.[8]

In A.D. 54, on the day Nero assumed the toga, there was an earthquake. Another earthquake is recorded as occurring in A.D. 60 in the city of Laodicea. The city was devastated along with its neighbors, Hierapolis and Colossae. Seneca wrote in A.D. 50,

> How often there have the cities of Asia and Achaea fallen with one fatal shock! How many cities have been swallowed up in Syria! How many in Macedonia! How often has Paphos become a ruin! News has often brought to us word of the demolition of whole cities as one.[9]

The city of Pompeii was destroyed in A.D. 63 by an earthquake. Josephus recorded a major quake in Judea.

> ". . . for there broke out a prodigious storm in the night, with the utmost violence, and very strong winds, with the largest showers of rain, with continual lightnings, terrible thundering, and amazing concussions and bellowings of the earth, that was in an earthquake. These things were a manifest indication that some destruction was coming upon men, when the system of the world was put into this disorder; and anyone would

---

[8] Tacitus, *Annuls of Tacitus*, Book V.
[9] de Botton, quoted in *The Consolations of Philosophy*.

guess that these wonders foreshowed some grand calamities that were coming."[10]

Additional Warnings

In addition to famines, pestilences, and earthquakes, Jesus warned His disciples of persecution and the rise of false prophets.

> "Then they will deliver you up to tribulation and kill you, and you will be hated by all nations for My name's sake. And then many will be offended, will betray one another, and will hate one another. Then many false prophets will rise up and deceive many. And because lawlessness will abound, the love of many will grow cold. But he who endures to the end shall be saved. And this gospel of the kingdom will be preached in all the world as a witness to all the nations, and then the end will come (Matt. 24:9–14).

> "But watch out for yourselves, for they will deliver you up to councils, and you will be beaten in the synagogues. You will be brought before rulers and kings for My sake, for a testimony to them. And the gospel must first be preached to all the nations. But when they arrest *you* and deliver you up, do not worry beforehand, or premeditate what you will speak. But whatever is given you in that hour, speak that; for it is not you who speak, but the

---

[10] Josephus, *Wars*, Book 4, Chapter 4:5.

Holy Spirit. Now brother will betray brother to death, and a father *his* child; and children will rise up against parents and cause them to be put to death. And you will be hated by all for My name's sake. But he who endures to the end shall be saved (Mark 13:9–13).

"But before all these things, they will lay their hands on you and persecute *you*, delivering *you* up to the synagogues and prisons. You will be brought before kings and rulers for My name's sake. But it will turn out for you as an occasion for testimony. Therefore settle *it* in your hearts not to meditate beforehand on what you will answer; for I will give you a mouth and wisdom which all your adversaries will not be able to contradict or resist. You will be betrayed even by parents and brothers, relatives and friends; and they will put *some* of you to death. And you will be hated by all for My name's sake. But not a hair of your head shall be lost. By your patience possess your souls (Luke 21:12–19).

Persecution

The two general dangers to the early church were the external danger of persecution and the internal threat of false prophets to deceive the people and to change the message of the Gospel. External persecution would come from two sources: the hostile Jewish community, and the official sanction of Roman oppression for political reasons.

At first the opposition to the Christian community was limited in nature and generated from local discontent (Acts 13:50–51; 14:18–19; 16:19–23; 17:1–10; 19:23–41). Then came the persecution authorized under the auspices of the civil or religious authorities (Acts 7:54–60; 8:1; 9:1; 23). After the city of Rome was destroyed by fire, the Neronian Persecution (A.D. 64–68) began in earnest.

Despite the hardship on the early church, Jesus limited the duration of the coming ordeal for His people to the period before A.D. 70. This fact is reflected in part by the reference the Lord made to the councils and to the synagogues in Mark 13:9 and Luke 21:12. And there was a blessing in disguise. Despite the trauma suffered by the early church, and as a direct result of the great tribulation, the Gospel was published among all nations as the Jews were dispersed from their ancestral homeland (Matt. 24:14; Mark 13:10; cf. 2 Tim. 4:17; Rom. 1:8; 16:26; and Col. 1:6, 23).

The Rise of False Prophets

As the early church had to endure persecution, it also had to combat heresies. Galatians, Colossians, 2 Corinthians, 2 Timothy, 2 Peter, 1 John and Jude were specifically written to counter the corrupting influence of false teachers and false doctrines. Almost all of the New Testament epistles contain some warning about the destructive impact of evil teachers who desired to infiltrate the church (1 Tim. 4:1–2; 2 Tim. 3:13; 4:3; 2 Pet. 2:1–3). With so much persecution so quickly, it seemed to many converts to Christ the world was coming to an end. The signs of the times indicated that

Christ was coming again soon, and the earth was to perish in divine judgment.

An Important Observation

At this point it is extremely important to read again Matthew 24:6, Mark 13:7 and Luke 21:9 for in these verses the church is reminded that Jesus cautioned His followers *not* to look at wars, the rise of false prophets, famines, pestilences or earthquakes as positive indications of the end of the world. "And you will hear of wars and rumors of wars. See that you are not troubled; for all *these things* must come to pass, but the end is not yet" (Matt. 24:6). Mark's Gospel reads, "But when you hear of wars and rumors of wars, do not be troubled; for *such things* must happen, but the end *is* not yet" (Mark 13:7). While Luke's Gospel records, "But when you hear of wars and commotions, do not be terrified; for these things must come to pass first, but the end *will* not *come* immediately" (Luke 21:9). Despite this divine prohibition, even to the people of His day, Christians have pointed time and again to contemporary events as ultimate proof of the end of this world. "But the end is not yet."

FEARFUL SIGHTS AND GREAT SIGNS

Since the fall of Jerusalem in A.D. 70, God's people should never be encouraged to look for sensational current events as fulfillment of biblical prophecy. God's people should not be taught to fear the future. God's people should be taught that between A.D. 30 and A.D. 70, during the days of God's vengeance upon the land of Israel, there were fearful sights and great signs, according to prophecy. Jesus said there would be. "And there will be great earthquakes in various places, and famines and pestilences; and there will be fearful sights and great signs from heaven" (Luke 21:11).

By "great signs" Jesus was most likely referring to the upheavals in nature that were catastrophic. Devastating storms, meteor showers, volcanic eruptions, and cyclones have always struck terror into the hearts of men. Josephus writes of several fearful sights that occurred prior to the destruction of Jerusalem.

> Thus were the miserable people persuaded by these deceivers, and such as belied God himself, while they did not attend, nor give credit, to the signs that were so evident and did so plainly foretell their future desolation; but, like men infatuated, without either eyes to see, or minds to consider, did not regard the denunciations that God made to them. Thus there was a star resembling a sword, which stood over the city, and a comet, that continued a whole year. Thus also, before the Jews rebellion, and before those commotions which preceded the war, when the people were come in great crowds to the feast of unleavened bread, on the eighth day of the month Xanthicus (Nisan), and at the ninth hour of the night, so great a light shone round the altar and the holy house, that it appeared to be bright day

time; which light lasted for half an hour. This light seemed to be a good sign to the unskilled, but was so interpreted by the sacred scribes, as to portend those events that followed immediately upon it.

At the same festival also, a heifer, as she was led by the high-priest to be sacrificed, brought forth a lamb in the midst of the temple. Moreover, the eastern gate of the inner (court of the) temple, which was of brass, and vastly heavy, and had been with difficulty shut by twenty men, and rested upon a basis armed with iron, and had bolts fastened very deep into the firm floor, which was there made of one entire stone, was seen to be opened of its own accord about the sixth hour of the night. Now, those that kept watch in the temple, and told him of it: who then came up thither, and not without great difficulty, was able to shut the gate again. This also appeared to the vulgar to be a very happy prodigy, as if God did thereby open them the gate of happiness. But the men of learning understood it, that the security of their holy house was dissolved of its own accord, and that the gate was opened for the advantage of their enemies. So these publicly declared, that this signal foreshowed the desolation that was coming upon them."[11]

---

[11] Josephus, *Wars*, Book 6, Chapter 5:3, 4.

The Specific Sign

As Jesus provided several general signs that would indicate the time of the coming judgment upon the generation to which He spoke (A.D. 30 – A.D. 70), He also provided a specific sign.

> When ye therefore shall see the abomination of desolation, spoken of by Daniel the prophet, stand in the holy place, (whoso readeth, let him understand:) Then let them which be in Judaea flee into the mountains: (Matt. 24:15–16).

> But when ye shall see the abomination of desolation, spoken of by Daniel the prophet, standing where it ought not, (let him that readeth understand,) then let them that be in Judaea flee to the mountains (Mark 13:14).

> And when ye shall see Jerusalem compassed with armies, then know that the desolation thereof is nigh. Then let them which are in Judaea flee to the mountains; and let them which are in the midst of it depart out; and let not them that are in the countries enter thereinto (Luke 21:20–21).

Three times Jesus told His disciples that something could be seen as a specific sign of the nearness of the fall of Jerusalem in the generation to which He spoke. What could be seen was the abomination of desolation spoken of by Daniel the prophet. Luke 21:20 specifically calls the abomination of desolation spoken of by Daniel the armies [of Rome]. When Jerusalem was encircled by the Roman legions the disciples of Christ would have a definite sign that was asked for as to the impending desolation of Jerusalem after which not one stone would be left on top of another. When the Roman legions finally subdued the city of Jerusalem in A.D. 70, history records the army brought their ensigns into the Temple, erected them over the Eastern Gate, and sacrificed to them proclaiming Titus as Emperor.

> And now the Romans, upon the flight of the seditious into the city, and upon the burning of the holy house itself, and of all the buildings round about it, brought their ensigns to the temple, and set them over against its eastern gate; and there did they offer sacrifices to them, and there did they make Titus Emperor, with the greatest acclamations of joy.[12]

The plain wording of Luke's account reveals the sign the disciples asked for and the Lord gave was to be clearly observed by the people of Jerusalem and Judea. "And when ye shall see Jerusalem compassed with armies . . . Then let them which are in Judaea flee" (Luke 21:20–21) said Jesus. Historian Philip Schaff recounts the Roman invasion of Jerusalem and how the armies were so positioned as to encircle the city. When the eagle banners were raised the prophecy of Jesus on this event was fulfilled.

---

[12] Josephus, *Wars*, Book 6, Chapter 6:1.

THE ROMAN INVASION

The emperor Nero, informed of the rebellion, sent his most famous general, Vespasian, with a large force to Palestine. Vespasian opened the campaign in the year A.D. 67 from the Syrian port-town, Ptolemais (Acco), and against a stout resistance over-ran Galilee with an army of sixty thousand men. But events in Rome hindered him from completing the victory, and required him to return thither. Nero had killed himself. The emperors, Galba, Otho, and Vitellius followed one another in rapid succession. The latter was taken out of a dog's kennel in Rome while drunk, dragged through the streets, and shamefully put to death. Vespasian, in the year 69, was universally proclaimed emperor, and restored order and prosperity. His son, Titus, who himself ten years after became emperor, and highly distinguished himself by his mildness and philanthropy, then undertook the prosecution of the Jewish war, and became the instrument in the hand of God of destroying the holy city and the temple. He had an army of not less than eighty thousand trained soldiers, and planted his camp on Mount Scopus and the adjoining Mount Olivet, in full view of the city and the temple, which from this height showed to the best advantage.

The valley of the Kedron divided the besiegers from the besieged. In April, A.D. 70, immediately after the Passover, when Jerusalem was filled with strangers, the siege began. The zealots rejected, with sneering defiance, the repeated proposals of Titus and the prayers of Josephus, who accompanied him as interpreter and mediator; and they struck down every one who spoke of surrender. They made sorties down from the valley of the Kedron and up the mountain, and inflicted great loss on the Romans. As the difficulties multiplied their courage increased. The crucifixion of hundreds of prisoners (as many as five hundred a day) only enraged them the more. Even the famine which began to rage and sweep away thousands daily, and forced a woman to roast her own child. The cries of mothers and babes, the most pitiable scenes of misery around them, could not move the crazy fanatics.

History records no other instance of such obstinate resistance, such desperate bravery and contempt of death. The Jews fought, not only for civil liberty, life, and their native land, but for that which constituted their national pride and glory, and gave their whole history its significance—for their religion, which, even in this state of horrible degeneracy, infused into them an almost superhuman power of endurance.[13]

---

[13] Schaff, *History of the Christian Church*, vol. 1, 395–396.

THE HISTORICAL RECORD

Here then is the historical record. The armies of Rome advanced against Jerusalem. The army encircled the city as it encamped on Mt. Scopus. The Roman banners were unfurled and the eagle was shown. The army of abomination that was to make the city desolate was present. It was then the Christians remembered the words of the Lord that this would be the sign to make their great escape.

> "Then let those who are in Judea flee to the mountains. Let him who is on the housetop not go down to take anything out of his house. And let him who is in the field not go back to get his clothes. But woe to those who are pregnant and to those who are nursing babies in those days! And pray that your flight may not be in winter or on the Sabbath (Matt. 24:16–20).

> "So when you see the 'abomination of desolation,' spoken of by Daniel the prophet, standing where it ought not" (let the reader understand), "then let those who are in Judea flee to the mountains. Let him who is on the housetop not go down into the house, nor enter to take anything out of his house. And let him who is in the field not go back to get his clothes. But woe to those who are pregnant and to those who are nursing babies

in those days! And pray that your flight may not be in winter (Mark 13:14-18).

Then let those who are in Judea flee to the mountains, let those who are in the midst of her depart, and let not those who are in the country enter her. For these are the days of vengeance, that all things which are written may be fulfilled. But woe to those who are pregnant and to those who are nursing babies in those days! For there will be great distress in the land and wrath upon this people (Luke 21:21–23).

A WAY OF ESCAPE

In order to protect the Church the Lord provided practical instruction as well as a specific sign. The signal that destruction was about to come upon Jerusalem in which the Temple would be destroyed would be the gathering of the armies of Rome around the city. Once the signal was seen the Christian community was to flee into the mountains. The flight must be without any prior preparations or excessive baggage. Prayer was to be requested for favorable weather and proper timing lest zealous Jews accuse the Christians of violating the Sabbath (Acts 21:20). History records that many within the Christian community escaped the destruction of Jerusalem in A.D. 70 by the Roman armies. At first, it appeared no one would escape Jerusalem for the events happened so suddenly.

When the Jewish Revolt broke out in A.D. 66 the Roman general Cestius Gallus moved his army from Syria into Judea with rapid deployment. The Roman assault was so swift the Christians along with all others were trapped within the city walls. They saw the sign as Jesus predicated but felt hopeless to escape. Then, without any warning or reason General Cestius Gallus recalled his soldiers and withdrew from the city.

> It then happened that Cestius was not conscious either how the besieged despaired of success, nor how courageous the people were for him; and so he recalled his soldiers from the place, and by despairing of any expectation of taking it, without having received any disgrace, he retired from the city, without any reason in the world.[14]

The surprise withdrawal provided the window of opportunity for the Christian community to escape according to the guidelines Christ provided. Eusebius (A.D. 263–339), the Christian historian, stated that, "The whole body . . . of the church at Jerusalem having been commanded by a divine revelation given to men of approved piety there before the war, removed from the city and dwelt at a certain town beyond the Jordan, called Pella."[15] "For then shall be great tribulation, such as was not since the beginning of the world to this time, no, nor ever shall be" (Matt. 24:21 KJV). "For in those days shall be affliction, such

---

[14] Josephus, *Wars*, Book 2, Chapter 19:7.
[15] Eusebius, *Ecclesiastical History*, 111, 5:3.

as was not from the beginning of the creation which God created unto this time, neither shall be" (Mark 13:19 KJV). "For these be the days of vengeance, that all things which are written may be fulfilled. But woe unto them that are with child, and to them that give suck, in those days! For there shall be great distress in the land, and wrath upon this people. And they shall fall by the edge of the sword, and shall be led away captive into all nations: and Jerusalem shall be trodden down of the Gentiles, until the times of the Gentiles be fulfilled" (Luke 21:22–24 KJV).

From A.D. 66–70, the stage was set for a period of great tribulation to engulf the Jewish nation as the cup of wrath of God was poured out on Israel for rejecting the Messiah (Matt. 23:32). These were "days of vengeance" (Luke 21:22–23). Of this period Josephus, who was an eyewitness wrote,

> ". . . it appears to me that the misfortunes of all men from the beginning of the world, if they be compared to those of the Jews, are not so considerable as they were . . . It is therefore impossible to go distinctly over every instance of these men's iniquity. I shall therefore speak my mind here at once briefly: That neither did any other city ever suffer such miseries, nor did any age ever breed a generation more fruitful in wickedness than this was, from the beginning of the world . . ."[16]

---

[16] Josephus, *Wars*, Book 5, Chapter 10:5.

Theologian Loraine Boettner comments on the degree of suffering the Jews endured in A.D. 70 with the fall of Jerusalem.

> Because of the horror of World War I and World War II it has been argued that the emphatic statement of Jesus in Matthew 24:21 and Mark 13:19, a statement confirmed by Josephus and others, have yet to be realized. Critics point to the numbers slain, the amount of property destroyed, the duration of time in suffering, and the extent of the geographical coverage of persecuted Jews in the 20th century and then declare that the words of Jesus have yet to be fulfilled. This commitment to simple numbers, how many bodies killed, how much money taken from the Jews in A.D. 70 compared to modem times misses the point of the words of Jesus to His generation. It is the *kind* of the days of vengeance that must be considered for in the period of the great tribulation (A.D. 30 to A.D. 70) there was nothing less than Almighty God divorcing His ancient wife who had proved unfaithful to Him. It was the time of Jacob's trouble (Jer. 30:7). It was the period of God concentrating His wrath upon His elect nation in particular (Luke 21:22–23; Dan. 12:1). There have been, of course, other periods of tribulation of suffering in which greater numbers of people were involved, and which continued for longer periods of time. But considering the physical, moral, and

religious aspects, suffering never reached a greater degree of awfulness and intensity than the siege of Jerusalem. Nor have so many people ever perished in the fall of any other city. We think of the atomic bomb that was dropped on Hiroshima as causing the greatest mass horror of anything in modern times. Yet, only about one tenth as many people were killed in Hiroshima as in the fall of Jerusalem. Add to the slaughter of such a great number the bestiality of Jew to Jew and of Roman to Jew and the anguish of a people who knew they were forsaken of God, and we see the justification for Christ's words, "For then shall be great tribulation, such as was not from the beginning of the world to this time, no, nor ever shall be." [17]

It is instructive that Josephus viewed the divine judgment on Jerusalem in A.D. 70 as a literal fulfillment of the prophet Daniel and so confirmed the prophecy of Jesus.

> In the very same manner Daniel also wrote concerning the Roman government, and that our country should be made desolate by them. All these things did this man leave in writing, as God had showed them to him, insomuch, that such as read his prophecies, and see how they have been fulfilled, would wonder at the wherewith God honored Daniel..."[18]

---

[17] Boettner, *The Millennium*.
[18] Josephus, *Antiquities*, Book 10, Chapter 11:7.

SHORTENED DAYS

Turning again to the parallel passages in Matthew 24, Mark 13, and Luke 21 there is found yet another prediction concerning the great tribulation Jesus envisioned for the people of His generation. So terrible would the time period be that God himself would have to intervene to shorten the days of divine discipline. Jesus promised the Father would do just that. "And unless those days were shortened, no flesh would be saved; but for the elect's sake those days will be shortened" (Matt. 24:22). "And unless the Lord had shortened those days, no flesh would be saved; but for the elect's sake, whom He chose, He shortened the days" (Mark 13:20).

The word "elect" signifies those precious souls who have been selected or chosen of God to be the heirs of salvation and the objects of special redeeming grace. The "elect" is a reference to the people of God and not to national Israel according to the flesh. The whole purpose of the divine judgment upon Israel was because of the wickedness of the unbelieving Jews in rejecting the Messiah. Those who did not reject the Messiah would know a special divine deliverance out of the great tribulation period of A.D. 40–70. The application of the word "elect" to the Christian community is manifested in the fact the warning was given about false Christ's and false prophets who would attempt to deceive the very elect if possible. History records the days Christ referred to were shortened by the divisions and fratricidal slaughter that took place within the city as well as the famines. Josephus notes that, "for barbarity and iniquity those of the same nation did in no way differ from the Romans; nay it seemed to be a much lighter thing to be ruined by the Romans than by themselves."[19]

William Kimball observes several other pertinent factors which contributed to shortening the duration of the siege: Titus was personally disposed to clemency and moderation towards the Jews, being in love with Agrippa's sister Bernice, as well as possessing great esteem towards Josephus the historian; Vespasian's attention had increasingly turned to Rome as the prospects of emperorship brightened; an outbreak of revolts on the northern frontiers of the Empire demanded immediate attention; and Titus, who had been left in charge of the Roman forces in Judea by Vespasian, was eager to return to Rome to share in the inaugural festivities of his father. The total duration of the final siege on Jerusalem lasted less than five months, from April to September of A.D. 70.[20]

God's intervention in those days is evidenced in that in an unexpected manner the Jewish strongholds were suddenly abandoned. Had the zealots maintained their position, they could have delayed the siege of Jerusalem indefinitely as the historian Josephus records.

> And here one may chiefly reflect on the power of God exercised upon these wicked wretches, and on the good fortune of the Romans; for these tyrants did now wholly deprive themselves of the security

---

[19] Josephus, *Wars*, Book 4, Chapter 3:2.
[20] Kimball, *The Great Tribulation*, 138.

they had in their own power, and came down from those very towers of their own accord, wherein they could have never been taken by force, nor indeed by any other way than by famine . . . So they now left these towers of themselves, or rather they were ejected out of them by God himself.[21]

Josephus contends that had General Gallus not withdrawn his troops he would have captured Jerusalem and spared the Temple. But then he concludes, "It was, I suppose, owing to the aversion God had already towards the city and the sanctuary, that he (Cestius) was hindered from putting an end to the war that very day."[22] Christ's warning was literally fulfilled by the church, allowing it to be delivered from most of the great tribulation that came to Jerusalem in A.D. 70. This prediction and its fulfillment exalt Christ in His prophetic role. The Lord is our wonderful King, Priest, and Prophet.

MORE WARNINGS OF FALSE DECEIVERS

In order to confirm the elect would be protected, not by a secret rapture or removal, but by the power of God, Jesus again warned about false prophets who would deceive the church by teaching of a secret, silent return of Christ.

> Then if anyone says to you, 'Look, here *is* the Christ!' or 'There!' do not believe *it*. For false christs and false prophets will rise and show great

---

[21] Josephus, *Wars*, Book 6, Chapter 8:4, 5.
[22] Ibid., *Wars*, Book 2, Chapter 19:6.

signs and wonders to deceive, if possible, even the elect. See, I have told you beforehand. "Therefore if they say to you, 'Look, He is in the desert!' do not go out; or 'Look, *He is* in the inner rooms!' do not believe *it*. For as the lightning comes from the east and flashes to the west, so also will the coming of the Son of Man be (Matt. 24:23–27).

"Then if anyone says to you, 'Look, here *is* the Christ!' or, 'Look, *He is* there!' do not believe it. For false christs and false prophets will rise and show signs and wonders to deceive, if possible, even the elect. But take heed; see, I have told you all things beforehand (Mark 13:21-23).

Despite the sensationalism of much modern prophetic teaching, the only time the Bible speaks of an imminent coming of Christ based on alleged signs, Jesus said, "believe it not."

THE VISIBLE COMING OF CHRIST

The destruction of Jerusalem with the far-reaching implications of that event was so monumental that Jesus repeated His words of warning to the disciples time and again. "See, I have told you beforehand" (Matt. 24:25). There would be false prophets and false teaching, said Jesus. In particular the Lord warned those would who presented a concept that His appearance would be cloaked in secrecy. Jesus asserted that His coming would be very conspicuous. "For as the lightning comes from the east and flashes to the west, so also will the coming of the Son of Man be" (Matt. 24:27).

One of the more popular, but erroneous, teachings in modern Christendom is the concept of a secret, silent coming of Christ whereby the Lord comes for His church and then seven years later returns to earth with His church. In light of the plain teaching of the Lord such a concept has to be reconsidered. The Lord will not return in secret, though, admittedly, He will come again like a thief in the night (1 Thess. 5:2; 2 Pet. 3:10) which only means He will come *suddenly* and *with overwhelming force*. But the Lord will come only a second time for all who believe (Heb. 9:28) and in the same manner in which He went away (Acts 1:11).

In Luke 21:24, Jesus continued to tell about the great tribulation that history records happened in A.D. 70. The proper understanding of this verse necessitates some specific points being made concerning the times of the Gentiles.

> And they will fall by the edge of the sword, and be led away captive into all nations. And Jerusalem will be trampled by Gentiles until the times of the Gentiles are fulfilled (Luke 21:24).

THE TIMES OF THE GENTILES

The expression *"the times of the Gentiles"* is found only in Luke's account of the Olivet Discourse (Luke 21:24). This phase immediately follows the Lord's announcement of the divine judgment which and did befall Jerusalem. The expression should not be divorced from the context of the outpouring of God's wrath upon the Jews. Though God would use the Gentile nations to judge His people, there would be a time limit to the act of discipline. Jesus had warned that such an event would take place. God would reject Israel and turn to the Gentiles (Matt. 8:11–12; Luke 13:28–29; Matt. 21:33–43; 22:2–7). The Apostle Paul declared that indeed God did shift the focus of His attention towards the Gentiles (Acts 13:46–47; 28:25–28). How long the Gentiles shall "trodden down" Jerusalem is uncertain and no one has the answer. There are no signs to indicate how long this period will continue.

Many people with prophetic interests were excited that Israel became a nation again in the eyes of the world community in 1948. The concept began to be taught once again that within a generation, Jesus would return. The prophetic teacher of the 1960s, '70s and even early '80s contended that since a biblical generation was approximately forty years in duration, the Lord would return, they said, by 1988. Some went even further in speculation and contended that since there was to be the great tribulation, seven years had to be subtracted and the secret coming of Christ would commence in 1981.

We know how that turned out!

Only one facet of modern day prophetic utterances has been constant: all of the prophetic teachers have been wrong in their predictions. In the Old Testament era death was the penalty for having prophesied in the name of the Lord in error. "But the prophet who presumes to speak a word in My name, which I have not commanded him to speak, or who speaks in the name of other gods, that prophet shall die" (Deut. 18:20). This is not to suggest that we should put to death those who falsely predict the Second Coming. Rather, only to illustrate there is a reason for such a harsh penalty. God did not, and does not, want His people to be afraid of the future based on erroneous teaching. "When a prophet speaks in the name of the LORD, if the thing does not happen or come to pass, that *is* the thing which the LORD has not spoken; the prophet has spoken it presumptuously; you shall not be afraid of him" (Deut. 18:22). Let the church rejoice, "For God has not given us a spirit of fear, but of power and of love and of a sound mind" (2 Timothy 1:7).

Not a few modern day prophetic teachers have also succumbed to the temptation to support their ever increasing novel theories with general date setting based upon the "signs" of the times, current events, or a personal "feeling" the end is near. Some dare to claim a special revelation or a "word from the Lord". There is also the constant focus upon contemporary events in the Middle East instead of the eternal Word of God. Many have taught the church to look for an alleged world dominating anti-Christ rather than the blessed day of the Lord. The Lord has stated there would come a time when the times of the Gentiles would be fulfilled. The church must simply wait upon God's timing to find out what that ultimately means.

Despite the severity of the great tribulation period, despite the long duration whereby Jerusalem would be trodden down by the Gentiles, the church of the generation of Jesus could at least be made aware when these things were about to begin to happen. "For wherever the carcass is, there the eagles will be gathered together" (Matt. 24:28).

THE CARCASS AND THE EAGLES

In very pictorial language Jesus used a familiar proverb of His day to emphasize that an event was coming which spoke of death and destruction. The picture of a carcass for national spiritual Israel was an appropriate description. Matthew Henry commented on this verse saying:

> The Jews were so corrupt and degenerate, so vile and vicious, that they were become a carcass, obnoxious to the righteous judgment of God; they were also so factious and seditious, and every way so provoking to the Romans, that they had made themselves obnoxious to their resentments, and an inviting prey to them . . . When a people (Jews) do by their sin make themselves carcasses, putrid and loathsome, nothing can be expected but that God should send eagles among them to devour and destroy them.[23]

It is interesting and instructive that the great emblem on the Roman banners was the eagle. As the Roman soldiers surrounded the city, as the banners were unfurled, it must have looked as if the eagles of the earth had gathered together to feed on the carcass of Jerusalem.

---

[23] Henry, *Commentary on the Whole Bible*, Matthew 24:4–31.

A TURBULENCE IN NATURE

In addition to the terrible carnage that would take place on earth, Jesus also foresaw turbulence in the sphere of nature. "Immediately after the tribulation of those days the sun will be darkened, and the moon will not give its light, and the stars will fall from heaven, and the powers of the heavens will be shaken" (Matt. 24:29). And Mark: "But in those days, after that tribulation, the sun will be darkened, and the moon will not give its light, and the stars will be falling from heaven, and the powers in the heavens will be shaken" (Mark 13:24–25). And Luke: "And there will be signs in sun and moon and stars, and upon the earth distress of nations in perplexity at the roaring of the sea and the waves, men fainting with fear and with foreboding of what is coming on the world; for the powers of the heavens will be shaken" (Luke 21:25–26).

4

After the Destruction of Jerusalem

Not only did Jesus predict the events leading up to and including the destruction of Jerusalem, but His prophetic eye saw those events that would follow in the immediate aftermath of Jerusalem's destruction. As the Great Prophet, the Lord Jesus stressed that Jerusalem would know a period of great tribulation but that its duration would be shortened. Then, "immediately" (Greek, *eutheōs*, "forthwith", "straightway", "shortly", "immediately") after those days there would be cataclysmic changes in the sun, moon, and stars.

The question arises whether or not these verses are to be taken literally or figuratively. There are several compelling reasons to attach a figurative meaning to these verses.

First, Jesus strictly discouraged the use of literal, cosmic events to be taken as signs proceeding His Second Advent (Matt. 24:6; Mark 13:7).

Second, no other section of the prophetic discourse is so indebted to scriptural imagery and language. "And there shall be signs" is language that goes beyond the limited period of the great tribulation period culminating in A.D. 70 to describe the conditions of earth until the times of the Gentiles are complete. There is no time in world history since our Lord spoke these words the thought would not be true. Therefore, these verses symbolically set forth the unsettled and turbulent state of the powers of the world. Henry Barclay Swete comments: "In all these cases, physical phenomena are used to describe the upheaval of dynasties, or great moral and spiritual changes, and it is unnecessary to exact any other meaning from the words when they are adopted by Christ."[24]

Third, in the Old Testament the prophets often used figurative language when depicting tumultuous times as the following passages teach. For example, Ecclesiastes 12:1 uses symbolic language to characterize the good times of life. Psalm 37:6 describes in figurative language the spiritual blessings that belong to those who trust in the Lord, as does Isaiah 60:20. "He shall bring forth your righteousness as the light, And your justice as the noonday" (Ps. 37:6). "Your sun shall no longer go down, Nor shall your moon withdraw itself; For the LORD will be your everlasting light, And the days of your mourning shall be ended" (Isa. 60:20).

Negative symbolic language was used by both the major and minor prophets as per Isaiah 5:30; 59:9–10: Amos 8:2–9; Ezekiel 34:12; Zephaniah 1:4, 15; Isaiah 5:30; and Jeremiah

---

[24] Swete, *Commentary on Revelation*, 19.

4:23–28; 13:16. Similar symbolic language used to describe the destruction of Jerusalem was also used by the prophet Joel.

> "And it shall come to pass afterward
> That I will pour out My Spirit on all flesh;
> Your sons and your daughters shall prophesy,
> Your old men shall dream dreams,
> Your young men shall see visions.
> And also on *My* menservants and on *My* maidservants
> I will pour out My Spirit in those days.
> "And I will show wonders in the heavens and in the earth:
> Blood and fire and pillars of smoke.
> The sun shall be turned into darkness,
> And the moon into blood,
> Before the coming of the great and awesome day of the LORD. (Joel 2:28–31).

However, on the day of Pentecost, Peter informed his audience they were witnessing the fulfillment of prophecy by Joel concerning the outpouring of the Holy Spirit (Joel 2:10; 2:28–31 compared to Acts 2:28–32).

When describing the turbulence among the Gentile nations, the prophets used symbolic language (Ezek. 30:1–26; 32:7–15; Isa. 34:4–10; 13:9–20 compare to Dan. 5:21–31).

Concerning the phrase, "the powers of heaven shall be shaken" (Luke 21:26), perhaps the best biblical commentary is found in Ephesians 6:12–13.

For we do not wrestle against flesh and blood, but against principalities, against powers, against the rulers of the darkness of this age, against spiritual *hosts* of wickedness in the heavenly *places*. Therefore take up the whole armor of God, that you may be able to withstand in the evil day, and having done all, to stand.

Apocalyptic language is used to describe God's judgment on Edom (Obad. 1–21). It was used to describe God's judgment on Moab (Jer. 48:1–47). It was used to describe God's judgment on Ammon (Jer. 9:26; 25:21; 49:6; Dan. 11:41; Amos 1:13; Zeph. 2:8–9).

The conclusion is that Matthew 24:29 contains familiar apocalyptic language the disciples of Jesus and His followers would have understood. The great tribulation that was to come upon Jerusalem and ensure its destruction *before* that particular generation passed away (Matt. 24:34), would bring in its aftermath cataclysmic changes.

5

The Sign of the Son of Man

The phrase "the sign of the Son of man in heaven" simply suggests that when Jesus comes, when Christ appears a second time, there will be nothing subtle or mysterious about the event. It will be manifestly obvious to all humanity. Everyone will know. There will be no doubt about what is happening. The Greek word translated as *appears* is *phaino,* and means "to be brought forth unto light," "to become evident," "to appear." Consider now the parallel Synoptic Gospel passages.

> Then the sign of the Son of Man will appear in heaven, and then all the tribes of the earth will mourn, and they will see the Son of Man coming on the clouds of heaven with power and great glory. And He will send His angels with a great sound of a trumpet, and they will gather together

His elect from the four winds, from one end of heaven to the other (Matt. 24:30–31).

Then they will see the Son of Man coming in the clouds with great power and glory. And then He will send His angels, and gather together His elect from the four winds, from the farthest part of earth to the farthest part of heaven (Mark 13:26–27).

Then they will see the Son of Man coming in a cloud with power and great glory (Luke 21:27).

A DIFFERENCE OF OPINION

Up to this point in the Gospel narrative of the Olivet Discourse in Matthew 24:1–28, conservative Bible scholars who embrace the historical understanding of the great tribulation period are united. However, at Matthew 24:29 individuals divide into two general positions. One position believes the verses to follow, Matthew 24:29–34, are a figurative reference to the *spiritual* coming judgment of Christ in power and judgment upon the nation of Israel in A.D. 70. The destruction of Jerusalem is in itself the sign of the Son of Man who is in heaven having ascended to His Father (Acts 1:9). The great tribulation causes all the tribes of the earth to mourn due to the Diaspora as people witness Christ coming in the clouds of heaven with power and great glory and judgment upon Israel (Dan. 7:13 cf. Rev. 1:7).

THE SIGN OF THE SON OF MAN

A second position contends that Jesus suddenly shifts His focus away from the realities the present generation would experience and instead begins to speak of His Second Advent proper whereby He returns the second time in personal glory and power (Acts 1:11 cf. Heb. 9:28).

Which position is more plausible?

The arguments in favor of the former position of applying these passages to the impending judgment of Christ upon the nation of Israel in A.D. 70 may be listed.

First, Christ warned the Sanhedrin on the eve of His crucifixion: "Jesus said to him, '*It is as* you said. Nevertheless, I say to you, hereafter you will see the Son of Man sitting at the right hand of the Power, and coming on the clouds of heaven.'" (Matt. 26:64). If Christ came in judgment upon national Israel in A.D. 70 then some of the Sanhedrin would have seen the words of Christ fulfilled.

Second, there is much Old Testament symbolism that speaks of the Lord as "coming" to a place. Genesis 11:5 says, "The LORD came down to see the city." The Scriptures speak of the Lord coming to men in their dreams (Gen. 20:3). In Exodus 3:8 we read, "I have come down to deliver them." The psalmist wrote, "He shall come down like rain upon the grass before mowing" (Ps. 72:6). David spoke of the Lord's assistance in battle saying, "the Lord . . . bowed the heavens . . . and came down . . . he delivered me" (Ps. 18:6–17 KJV). The prophet Isaiah stated, "So the LORD of hosts will come down To fight for Mount Zion and for its hill" (Isa. 31:4). In the context of Israel's restoration to their homeland after the Babylonian captivity, God said, "I am returned unto Jerusalem" (Zech. 1:16; 8:3). There is a sense in which the Lord came to Israel in a great and terrible judgment in A.D. 70. Matthew Henry wrote what many Christians believe:

> The destruction of Jerusalem was in a particular manner an act of Christ's judgment, the judgment committed to the Son of man . . . it might justly be looked upon as a coming of the Son of man, in power and great glory, yet not visible in the clouds.[25]

Third, there are select passages to support the concept of a judgment upon national Israel in A.D. 70 which would include Exodus 19:9; 34:5; Isaiah 19:1; Psalm 18:10; Psalm 104:3, and Psalm 97:2.

Despite these compelling arguments for a spiritual and literal fulfillment of prophecy with the fall of Jerusalem in A.D. 70, there are conservative, godly scholars who prefer to understand the verses in Matthew 24:29–31, Mark 13:26–27, and Luke 21:27 as a direct reference to the Second Advent of Christ. The angels, the gathering of the elect, the coming in clouds, argues, say the advocates of this position, for an understanding of the Second Advent proper. Parallel New Testament passages offered for consideration in support of a still future view of prophetic events includes 1 Thessalonians 4:16; 1 Corinthians 15:52; and 2 Thessalonians 1:7.

---

[25] Henry, *Commentary on the Whole Bible*, Matthew 24:4–31.

A POSSIBLE SOLUTION

If there is a solution as to which position may be correct in its interpretation, the solution might be found in the word "then" of Matthew 24:30, Mark 13:26, and Luke 21:27. The word used in these verses is derived from the Greek *tote*. Matthew uses this word often, about ninety times, for something that happened subsequent in time. Therefore, the completion of this passage would be found in the events of A.D. 70. However, the word *tote* is flexible in that it can either indicate something that is to happen at a specific time, or it can be used in a far more general sense to indicate an event or series of events that will happen.

IN THE VALLEY OF DECISION
THE HISTORICAL FULFILLMENT VIEW

Advocates for a historical fulfillment of Matthew 24:30–31, Mark 13:26–27, and Luke 21:27 argue for the following order of events.

First, as Jesus predicted, a period of general hardship was to come upon the nation of Israel.

Second, this general turbulent period was to be followed by a span of time, of forty years characterized by increasing unrest and instability among the nations of the earth until "the times of the Gentiles" were complete.

Third, when the times of the Gentiles were completed, national Israel would mourn as the people viewed the Son of Man coming in great tribulation judgment, which He did in A.D. 70.

Fourth, the elect, consisting of the Christian community, would largely be spared. History records the visible church, consisting of the elect of God who remembered the words of Jesus, was spared most of the great, final judgment upon Jerusalem.

IN THE VALLEY OF DECISION
THE FUTURISTIC FULFILMENT VIEW

In contrast, advocates of the position that applies Matthew 24:30–31, Mark 13:26–27, and Luke 21:27 to the Second Advent of Christ would argue for the following order of events.

First, a great tribulation period is yet to come upon the nation of Israel.[26]

Second, this coming tribulation period is to be followed by an extended period of time, characterized by unrest and instability among the nations of the earth, which will end in great tribulation upon Israel.

Third, the future great tribulation period will be brought to a close with the Second Advent of Christ in power and glory as the Lord is accompanied with trumpets, angels, and the gathering of the elect.

Because individuals hold strongly to their respective positions, the discussion continues as to the exact meaning and the proper place in history to apply the events as

---

[26] The rapture of the church, initially taught in the nineteen century, is a theological construct associated with Dispensational teachings. Various positions contend that either prior to, during, or after a period of great tribulation, for Israel in particular and the world in general, the Lord will come to "rapture", or remove, the church. The Dispensationalist finds biblical support for this idea in 1 Thessalonians 4:16ff.

recorded in Matthew 24:30–31, Mark 13:26–27, and Luke 21:27.

THE DRAWING NEAR OF REDEMPTION!

Luke 21:28 returns to a definite, historical understanding of the text because Jesus told the disciples that when all the things He had just spoken of came to pass, they were to lift up their heads because their redemption was drawing near. "Now when these things begin to happen, look up and lift up your heads, because your redemption draws near" (Luke 21:28).

"LIFT UP YOUR HEADS"

The reference to "these things" (Luke 21:28 cf. Matt. 24:34) have led to speculation among some Bible teachers that a nexus should be made with the catastrophic upheavals and cosmic events which, they contend, will accompany the Second Advent. There are two major problems with such a connection.

First, there are no signs for the Second Advent of Christ (Matt. 24:36; Mark 13:33). Jesus said pointedly that *no person* would know the nearness of His return. The word for "know" in Greek is *eido* and means "to know, to be sure of, aware of, perceive, see, understand, tell, or to know from observation." Jesus actually meant it. No person will be able to clearly distinguish, perceive, be sure of, be aware of, or be able to know for certain when the Lord shall return the second time for all that believe (Heb. 9:28). The words,

"And when these things begin to come to pass," must be linked to those events Christ taught about when referring to the destruction of Jerusalem in A.D. 70. Without this understanding the words of Jesus would have had no meaning or discernment to the disciples' question concerning the destruction of the Temple which began the Olivet Discourse.

For the rest of the Christian community after A.D. 70, the church has always lived in the consciousness that "the end of all things is at hand" (Phil. 4:5 KJV; Jas. 5:9; 1 Pet. 4:7a). To the church Jesus says, "Do not be terrified," or, as the King James Version renders it, "Be not afraid" (Luke 21:9). While Christians travel through this life they have a hopeful expectancy "in the present age, looking for the blessed hope and glorious appearing of our great God and Savior Jesus Christ" (Titus 2:12–13).

6

Instruction from a Parable

THE PARABLE OF THE FIG TREE

There is another issue that should be briefly addressed relating to the Olivet Discourse which is the matter of Israel and the fig tree. Jesus ends his teaching with these words.

> "Now learn this parable from the fig tree: When its branch has already become tender and puts forth leaves, you know that summer *is* near. So you also, when you see all these things, know that it is near—at the doors! Assuredly, I say to you, this generation will by no means pass away till all these things take place. Heaven and earth will pass away, but My words will by no means pass away (Matt. 24:32–35).

"Now learn this parable from the fig tree: When its branch has already become tender, and puts forth leaves, you know that summer is near. So you also, when you see these things happening, know that it is near—at the doors! Assuredly, I say to you, this generation will by no means pass away till all these things take place. Heaven and earth will pass away, but My words will by no means pass away. (Mark 13:28-31).

Then He spoke to them a parable: "Look at the fig tree, and all the trees. When they are already budding, you see and know for yourselves that summer is now near. So you also, when you see these things happening, know that the kingdom of God is near. Assuredly, I say to you, this generation will by no means pass away till all things take place. Heaven and earth will pass away, but My words will by no means pass away (Luke 21:29–33).

ISRAEL AND THE FIG TREE

Dispensationalism has been universally identified by a belief that national Israel has a future that is distinct from that of the church.[27] It is widely taught throughout Christendom that "the budding of the fig tree" passage in Matthew 24:32 has a distinct and direct prophetic link to the re-establishment of Israel as a Jewish statehood among the

---

[27] Sawyer, *The Survivor's Guide to Theology*, 384.

community of modern nations in 1948 and the end of the world. The belief is propagated that since Israel became a nation, the end of time as it is now known is near and the present generation must be in the terminal generation that shall see the Second Advent of Christ first for His church and seven years later with His church.

In spite of the widespread popularity of this opinion being advanced in prophetic seminars and in facetious works such as the *Left Behind* series, there is absolutely no biblical support to teach people that individuals in a specific century constitute the terminal generation. All Christians want the Lord to return, but a holy longing does not mean a divine certainty. A biblical generation of forty years has already passed and the church is still on earth and the Lord has not returned the second time.

To the people of His day, the Lord taught a very simple truth using the fig tree and "all the trees" (Luke 21:29) as an object lesson. When trees put forth their leaves people know that summer is near. Likewise, when the disciples of the first generation witnessed all "these things" of the Olivet Discourse then they would know the Lord's prophetic utterances were about to be fulfilled. Alfred Edersheim recaptures the visual impact of the Lord's teaching at that moment in history.

> From the fig tree, under which, on that spring afternoon they may have rested on the Mount of Olives, they were to "learn a parable." We can picture Christ taking one of its twigs, just as its

softening tips were bursting into young leaf. Surely, this meant that summer was nigh—not that it had actually come. The distinction is important. For it seems to prove that 'all these things' which were to indicate to them that it was near, even at the doors, and which were to be fulfilled when this generation had passed away, could not have referred to the last signs connected with the immediate Advent of Christ, but must apply to the previous predication of the destruction of Jerusalem, and of the Jewish commonwealth.[28]

The single, penetrating, powerful thought that should crystallize all discussion concerning the great tribulation is that Jesus said to those who were listening to Him speak, "this generation shall not pass, till all these things be fulfilled" (Matt. 24:34; Luke 21:32). The disciples had asked when the events would come to pass the Lord had mentioned. Jesus said all the prophesied events would happen in "this generation," the generation to which He lived in and the generation that rejected Him as Lord. The disciples understood, and so can the church. By A.D. 70, the old city of Jerusalem and the Second Temple were destroyed so the spiritual nature of the kingdom of God could be made manifest.

A new Temple was created. This new Temple of God is the church. The kingdom of God that is spiritual and eternal

---

[28] Edersheim, *The Life and Times of Jesus the Messiah*, 650.

replaced the Jewish concept of a natural and temporal kingdom of God. Because of this great work of judgment of God upon national Israel in A.D. 70, it would be proper for the Christian community not to encourage Jewish materialistic expectations. The Lord has disciplined national Israel (Rom. 9—11). The Bible teaches that Christ loves the church and died for her (Eph. 5:25). It is the church, the true spiritual Israel of God (Gal. 3:29), which has a glorious destiny for He has made Christians kings and priests. Christ Jesus has made Christians kings and priests now (Rev. 1:6)! Christians are citizens of the kingdom of Christ and of that kingdom there shall be no end (Isa. 9:7; Luke 1:33). Here is comfort for people who have been taught to fear the future. Do not be afraid. The King has come. Come to the kingdom. "Believe on the Lord Jesus Christ, and you will be saved" (Acts 16:31).

7

An Important Doctrine

WHAT ABOUT ESCAPING TRIBULATION?

Since so much has been made within the Christian community about the possibility of God's people escaping a future great tribulation period by removal in an event popularly called the Rapture, it would be good to remember that God has never promised the church as a whole would ever be excluded from the trials of life. Consider the following teaching.

DOCTRINE OF TRIBULATION

(1) The word "tribulation" is found twenty-two times in the Authorized Version. The word "tribulations" is found four times.

(2) To suffer tribulation (Greek, *thlipsis*) is to suffer affliction, to be troubled, to suffer due to the pressure of circumstances, or the antagonism of persons.

(3) In examining the passages that speak of tribulation it becomes evident that God's people in all ages have known emotional, spiritual, and physical affliction (Deut. 4:30; Jdgs. 10:14; 1 Sam. 10:19; 26:24; Matt. 13:21).

(4) Tribulation also comes to those who are not God's people in the form of Divine discipline (Matt. 24:21, 29; Mark 13:24; 2 Thess. 1:6; Rom. 2:9, 22).

(5) Of particular concern is the Christian and tribulation. The Bible makes clear the followers of Christ, for as long as they are in the world, shall experience tribulation (John 16:33).

(6) Only through much tribulation will the saints enter into the kingdom (Acts 14:22).

(7) The value of tribulation is that it works patience (Rom. 5:3; 12:12).

(8) To undergo tribulation does not mean or imply a believers is loved less by Christ (Rom. 8:35), for nothing shall separate the believer from His faithful love.

(9) God finds a special way to comfort the saints who suffer tribulation (2 Cor. 1:4).

(10) Paul could find reasons to rejoice in the very midst of tribulation (2 Cor. 7:4; Rom. 5:3; 2 Thess. 1:4) and therefore did not want anyone else to worry on his behalf (Eph. 3:13).

(11) When believers at Thessalonica were surprised at the suffering they had to endure, Paul reminded them he had taught that Christians must suffer (1 Thess. 3:4).

(12) John, on the isle of Patmos, does not divorce himself from tribulation nor does he ever say of himself that he represents those who shall not suffer tribulation. On the contrary, John considers himself, at the moment of his writing, to be a companion in suffering (Rev. 1:9).

(13) The tribulation of the saints is well known to the Lord and is for a stated purpose (Revelation 2:9, 10).

(14) Historically, God's people have always emerged victorious out of tribulation no matter how great the trials might be (Rev. 7:14).

(15) There is not a single biblical passage that clearly and simply teaches God will spare His people from the purifying effects of tribulation, especially through rapture. Just the opposite is stated and demonstrated time and again.

(16) The story of the Old Testament, the writing of the New Testament, the documentation of two millennia of history testify to the blood of the saints in the church.

(17) Any teaching which seeks to exempt God's people from tribulation during any period of human history will not find support from the twenty-six passages which uses this word.

IS THE CHURCH IN THE BOOK OF THE REVELATION?

Unfortunately, a large part of the Christian community is being taught the church will not go through a special period of great tribulation which is believed by many to be in the future. In contrast, history records the specific great tribulation period Jesus predicted did find the Christian community caught up in the turmoil of the times. The Lord made a way of escape, not by rapture, but by the revelation of His word remembered. The Word of God plainly teaches tribulation for the saints until the Second Advent of Christ (Acts 14:22; Heb. 9:28). The testimony of the church down to the present hour confirms the saints are often persecuted and killed for the cause of Christ.

There is a clever and popular argument used to try to prove the church is not going to go through a great tribulation period by appealing to the book of the Revelation.

First, it is taught the events of Revelation 4—19 are future, not historical.

Second, it is argued the church could not have part in any great tribulation period because the word church is not found in the text of Revelation 4—19.

Third, a conclusion is drawn that since the church is not mentioned in Revelation 4—19 the church is not part of the great tribulation period.

Despite the success of this argument to the minds of many, the simple biblical response to this erroneous teaching is the truth: the church is found in the questionable chapters of Revelation 4—19. This is easily proved by observing the terminology used for the church in the Gospel of Matthew through Jude's epistle and then noting the same terminology is found in the book of Revelation.

TERMONOLOGY FOR THE CHURCH IN MATTHEW—JUDE COMPARED TO REVELATION 4—19

Saints	Saints
Romans 1:7	Revelation 14:12
1 Corinthians 1:2	Revelation 15:3
Ephesians 1:1	Revelation 17:6
Fellowservants	**Fellowservants**
Colossians 4:11	Revelation 6:11
Colossians 1:7	
Brethren	**Brethren**
1 Thessalonians 1:4	Revelation 6:11

Brethren	Brethren
Colossians 1:2	
2 Thessalonians 1:3	
People washed in the blood	People washed in the blood
1 Corinthians 6:11	Revelation 17:14
Called, chosen by God, faithful	Called, chosen by God, faithful
Ephesians 1:4	Revelation 17:14
2 Thessalonians 2:13	
The servant of Jesus	His servants
Ephesians 6:6	Revelation 19: 2, 5
Philippians 1:1	
Those who sleep in the Lord	Dead who died in the Lord
1 Thessalonians 4:14	Revelation 14:13
Prophets	Prophets
1 Corinthians 12:28	Revelation 16:6
1 Corinthians 14:29	
1 Corinthians 14:32	
Ephesians 2:20	

A LOGICAL CONCLUSION

It would be inconsistent to use the same terminology for "the church" in Revelation 4—19 that is found in the rest of the New Testament and then deny the church exists on earth during the great tribulation period Jesus spoke of and John saw visualized. Too much has been made over the absence of a specific term for the church (Greek, *ekklesia*), while ignoring the many other references to the church in Revelation 4—19.

If the absence of the specific term for the church, *ekklesia*, means the message of the Word of God does not speak of, or to, the church directly, then other books of the Bible must also be for some future generation than the present people of God because the specific terminology, *ekklesia*, is not found in the text. The word translated as "church" is found nowhere in the Gospel of Mark, the Gospel of Luke, John, 2 Peter, 1 John, 2 John, or Jude! Of course no one would suggest these books be discarded as not speaking directly to the church simply because a specific term is not found.

In like manner, the message of the Revelation is said to be for the church, especially the seven churches of Asia. The message of the Revelation is simple and precious. By way of interpretation the message of the Revelation spoke of impending judgment upon Israel. By way of application, an eternal principle is established. Any false prophet or beast that shall rise to hurt the church shall be destroyed. The Beast of Revelation 13, Nero, fell to the conquering Christ. While the Lord will judge His people, He will also move to protect His own.

The conclusion of studying the words of Jesus in Matthew 24, Mark 13 and Luke 21 is profound. The great tribulation period Jesus referred to is a historical reality. Once it was future, but fulfillment came in A.D. 70, as Jesus predicted. There is no reason for prophetic pundits to teach God's people to fear the future by postulating a future great tribulation period on the same magnitude and scale as what happened in A.D. 70. What should be taught instead is that when Christians do suffer normal tribulation or pressures, the Lord will be present to comfort, to guide, and to bless His own.

"'Comfort, yes, comfort My people!'" Says your God" (Isa. 40:1).

Appendix 1

Doctrine of the Coming of Christ

(1) Jesus said there would be some standing before Him who would not taste of death until they saw the Son of Man coming in His kingdom (Matt. 16:28; Luke 21:27).

(2) On the Mount of Olives the disciples asked the Lord for the sign of His coming (Matt. 24:3).

(3) Jesus likened His coming (Greek, *parousia*, advent, physical aspect or presence) to the lightning which cometh out of the east and shineth unto the west (Matt. 24:27).

(4) Jesus said there would be days of tribulation in which the sun would be darkened and the moon would not give her light and the powers of the heavens would be shaken and people would see the Son of Man coming (Greek, *kataggeleus*, a proclaimer, setter forth) in the clouds of

heaven with power and great glory (Matt. 24:30; Mark 13:26; Luke 21:26–27).

(5) The coming of the Son of Man would be like the days of Noah (Matt. 24:37, 39; Mark 13:36).

(6) Only evil servants would say, "My lord delayeth his coming" (Matt. 24:37, 39; Mark 13:36).

(7) Faithful servants are rewarded when the Lord comes again (Matt. 24:26).

(8) In a parable Jesus told what He would expect at His coming (Matt. 26:64; Mark 14:62).

(9) Jesus told the high priest that he would see the Son of Man sitting on the right hand of power and coming in the clouds of heaven (Matt. 26:64; Mark 14:62).

(10) Peter referred to the coming of the Just One (Acts 7:52), associating the prophetic reference to the First Advent.

(11) Paul speaks of the saints waiting for the coming (Greek, *apokalupsis*, revelation, manifestation) of the Lord (1 Cor. 1: 7).

(12) At the coming, at the *parousia* of Christ there will be the resurrection from the dead (1 Cor. 15:23).

(13) Paul wanted others to be present at the coming of Christ so he could rejoice (1 Thess. 2:19).

(14) When Christ comes the saints will be sanctified (1 Thess. 3:13).

(15) There will be a generation of saints at the coming of Christ who will meet Him in the air (1 Thess. 4:15).

(16) Sanctification—the process of becoming more like Jesus—must characterize the life of every Christian until the coming of Christ (1 Thess. 5:23).

(17) The hope of the coming of Christ becomes a motivating force for faithful service (2 Thess. 2: 1).

(18) The Wicked One will be destroyed at the coming of Christ (2 Thess. 2:8).

(19) Christians are to be patient in the hardships of life until the coming of the Lord (Jas. 5:7).

(20) The coming, the *parousia*, is near (Jas. 5:8).

(21) Skeptics mock that Jesus is coming again (2 Peter 3:4).

(22) When Jesus comes the heavens shall be set on fire and dissolved and the elements shall melt (2 Pet. 3:12).

(23) The Christian is to live in such a manner as not to be ashamed before Christ at His coming (1 John 2:28).

(24) Of the sixty six times the word "coming" is used in the New Testament, fourteen times the word is directly associated without question to the Second Advent of Christ (Heb. 9:28 cf. 1 Cor. 1:7; 15:23; 1 Thess. 2:19; 3:13; 4:15; 5:23; 2 Thess. 2:1; 2:8; Jas. 5:7; 5:8; 2 Pet. 1:16; 3:4; 3:12; 1 John 2:28). In four other passages there is a parabolic application (Matt. 24:48; 25:27; Luke 12:45; 19:23).

(25) The passages in Matthew (16:28; 24:27; 24:30; 24:37, 38, 39; 25:27) Mark (13:26, 36; 14:62), and Luke (21:27) may better refer to the coming of Christ in special judgment upon national Israel in A.D. 70.

(26) In the Old Testament the word "coming" is used 33 times.

(27) Only in Malachi 3:2 and 4:5 is the word "coming" associated with the Messiah.

(28) Malachi 3:2, which speaks of the Lord coming suddenly to His Temple, is fulfilled in Matthew 3:1, 3 (Rev. 6:17 cf. Heb. 12:29).

(29) Malachi 4:5 refers to the prophet Elijah coming before the great and dreadful day of the Lord. This coming is associated with the First Advent. Matthew 11:14 plainly

teaches the fulfillment of this prophetic utterance in the life of John the Baptist.

Appendix 2

The Greatest Prophecy Ever Fulfilled (A Study of Daniel 9:24-27)[29]

"Seventy weeks are determined upon thy people and upon thy holy city, to finish the transgression, and to make an end of sins, and to make reconciliation for iniquity, and to bring in everlasting righteousness, and to seal up the vision and prophecy, and to anoint the most Holy. Know therefore and understand, that from the going forth of the commandment to restore and to build Jerusalem unto the Messiah the Prince shall be seven weeks, and three score and two weeks: the street shall be built again, and the wall, even in troublous times. And after three score and two weeks shall Messiah be cut off, but not for himself: and the people of the prince that shall come shall destroy the city and the sanctuary; and the end thereof shall be with a flood, and unto the end of the

---

[29] All Scripture quotations in Appendix 2 are taken from the King James Version.

war desolations are determined. And he shall confirm the covenant with many for one week: and in the midst of the week he shall cause the sacrifice and the oblation to cease, and for the overspreading of abominations he shall make it desolate, even until the consummation, and that determined shall be poured upon the desolate" (Dan. 9:24–27).

INTRODUCTION

In order to appreciate prophecy, it must be kept in mind that the prophets did not express their own personal views. The Bible states plainly that the prophets told what God the Holy Spirit instructed them to tell.

"For the prophecy came not in old time by will of man, but holy men of God spake as they were moved by the Holy Ghost" (2 Pet. 1:21).

All the prophecies concerning Christ were fulfilled, including those given by Daniel.

"And he said unto them, These are the words which I spake unto you, while I was yet with you, that all things must be fulfilled, which were written in the law of Moses, and in the prophets, and in the psalms, concerning me" (Luke 24:44).

In Daniel's vision of seventy weeks, the weeks stand for years to total four hundred and ninety (490) years. The first sixty-nine (69) weeks measure a period of four hundred and eighty three (483) years, followed by the seventieth (70th) week of year or seven (7) years for a total of four hundred and ninety (490) years.

Since the first sixty-nine (69) weeks were literally fulfilled by the return of the Jews from Babylon to Israel to rebuild the city of Jerusalem, there is no compelling reason to believe that the final week is not also fulfilled, and that it naturally followed the 69th week in chronological order.

There is no time gap indicated in the Scriptural narrative. There is a theory that a time gap exists. A theory, according to Webster's dictionary, is an unproven assumption, or a hypothesis accepted for the sake of argument.

It has been suggested that a "Prophetic Time Clock" stopped at the end of the sixty-ninth (69th) week of years, or after 483 years.

The purpose of this alleged time stoppage is so that national Israel can, in the future, experience the seventieth (70th) week in the form of a special period called "The Great Tribulation."

It is argued that one day national Israel (and the whole world), shall suffer for seven (7) years, while being deceived by an anti-Christ, who will lead the world into the greatest battle of human history called, Armageddon.

It must be noted that none of these terrible events are mentioned in the text of Daniel 9.

The basic question of concern is this: "Did the 70th week follow the 69th week?"

If the seventieth (70th) week did follow the sixty-ninth (69th) week, then the "Postponement Theory", and the "Prophetic Clock" concept, and all other imagined events, can be exchanged for the simplicity of the Word of God, which lives and abides forever.

It is significant to note that Christendom did not know until the nineteenth and twentieth centuries the idea that the seventh week could be separated from the first sixty nine weeks by a period of more than two thousand years.

In contrast to the recently developed spectacular theories is God's specific, ancient, wording to Daniel, which was that, "seventy weeks are determined." This divine decree, in context, does not allow the separation of one week from the initial sixty-nine (69) weeks by a long period of time.

A comparison of this passage can be made with other time passages in scripture.

Item. When the prophecy of Christ was made that He was to be buried and rise again on the third day, there was no other day that the Lord could have risen and still fulfilled prophecy.

Item. When Joseph prophesied of seven fat years followed by seven years of famine, there was no indeterminate time between fulfillments.

Item. When Jeremiah prophesied of seventy years captivity in Babylon, it all happened on schedule, with one year following the next for seventy years. The seventieth year did not find fulfillment hundreds of years later.

God keeps His appointments on schedule. A break, or long postponement in prophecy, does not make a fulfillment possible according to the provisions of the Law.

"When a prophet speaketh in the name of the Lord, if the thing follow not, nor come to pass, that is the thing which the Lord hath not spoken, but the prophet hath spoken it presumptuously: thou shalt not be afraid of him" (Deut. 18:22).

Notice that there are no postponements permitted. A prophecy must come to pass within a specified time period to authenticate the prophet. Jesus Himself said that the Scriptures cannot be broken. "If he called them gods, unto whom the word of God came, and the scripture cannot be broken" (John 10:35).

A careful examination of Daniel 9:24–27 reveals that the prophet wrote about the consummation of God's plan for national Israel, not its national exaltation, and eventual restoration to dominate the other nations on earth.

To be specific, Daniel was told of many things that would happen to the Jews, and to the Holy City following the Babylonian Captivity. It was decreed that Jerusalem was to be restored (9:25) "for the street shall be built again, and the wall even in troublous times." The account of this work of rebuilding Jerusalem is given in the books of Ezra and Nehemiah.

Following the seventy years of Babylonian Captivity, God determined to restore Israel back to her land for at least four hundred and ninety more years, as reflected in the prophecy. The "weeks of years" principle can be found in other passages.

"After the number of the days in which ye searched the land, even forty days, each day for a year, shall ye bear your iniquities, even forty years, and ye shall know my breach of promise" (Num. 14:34).

Lie thou also upon thy left side, and lay the iniquity of the house of Israel upon it: according to the number of the days that thou shalt lie upon it thou shalt bear their iniquity. For I have laid upon thee the years of their iniquity, according to the number of the days, three hundred and ninety days: so shalt thou bear the iniquity of the house of Israel. And when thou hast accomplished them, lie again on thy right side, and thou shalt bear the iniquity of the house of Judah forty days: I have appointed thee each day for a year (Ezek. 4:4–6).

In that four hundred and ninety year period, important events would take place in the history of national Israel. Some of these events would be good, and some would be bad.

First, it was determined that Israel "would finish the transgression." The transgression of Israel had for a long time been the focus of the messages from God's prophets. It was for their transgressions that the Jews in the northern kingdom of Israel had gone into national captivity in 721 B.C. under the Assyrians. In 586 B.C. the southern kingdom of Judah fell to the Babylonians. It was for Jewish transgressions that the land of Palestine had been made desolate for seventy years. Daniel himself had confessed this by saying: "Yea, all have transgressed thy law, even by departing, that they might not obey thy voice; therefore, the curse is poured upon us" (Dan. 9:11).

As sad as this was, the angel Gabriel revealed to Daniel the distressing news that, as badly as Israel had behaved in the past, she would yet sin again to an even greater extent. Yes, Israel would be restored to her land following the seventy years in Babylon. Yes, the Holy Temple would be rebuilt.

Yes, the wall of the holy city Jerusalem would be made secure once more, but only so that the full measure of Israel's transgression might be made complete. It was to be the fate of the nation that the Messiah would come, only to be killed by a mindless Jewish mob.

Turning to the New Testament, we read that the Messiah did come to Israel. Jesus knew what Daniel had said, and the other prophets as well. After bringing a railing accusation against the Jewish leaders, the Lord said, "Fill ye up the measure of your fathers . . . that upon you may come all the righteous blood shed upon the earth" (Matt. 23:32).

With these words Jesus declared that the hour had come in His day for Israel to "finish the transgression" of rejecting all the words of warning, all of the prophets, all the means of grace, even to that which was offered by the Messiah. There would be a terrible price to pay by Israel for the transgression. Jesus predicted an awful doom upon the beloved city and its people. "Verily I say unto you, All these things shall come upon this generation" (Matt. 23:36).

When Jesus said, "this generation", He was speaking to the people of His day, not a generation of Jews thousands of years in the future.

Again, the Lord said, "Behold, your house is left unto you desolate" (Matt. 23:38). When the transgression of the Jewish nation was finished, as predicted by Daniel, then was brought to pass the words spoken by Peter on the day of Pentecost concerning Christ.

"Him, being delivered by the determinate counsel and foreknowledge of God, ye have taken, and by wicked hands have crucified and slain" (Acts 2:33).

Paul confirms that the crucifixion of Christ was the crowning sin of Israel, adding that the wrath of God would come upon Israel to the uttermost. The wrath of God did come. The year was A.D. 70. Jerusalem was destroyed. The Holy Temple was laid waste. The blood sacrifices were made to cease, and the Jewish people were scattered among the nations of the earth.

> Who both killed the Lord Jesus, and their own prophets, and have persecuted us; and they please not God, and are contrary to all men: Forbidding us to speak to the Gentiles that they might be saved, to fill up their sins alway: for the wrath is come upon them to the uttermost (1 Thess. 2:15).

Israel had broken her covenant vow. Israel had tried to kill her Husband. Israel had committed spiritual fornication.

Finally, the transgression completed, the Lord gave the true kingdom covenant blessing to a nation bringing forth the fruits of Christ, which Peter declares to be the true Israel of God, the *church* of the living God.

"Therefore say I unto you, The kingdom of God shall be taken from you, and given to a nation bringing forth the fruits thereof" (Matt. 21:43).

"But ye are a chosen generation, a royal priesthood, an holy nation, a peculiar people; that ye should shew forth the praises of him who hath called you out of darkness into his marvellous light" (1 Pet. 2:9).

Second, returning to Daniel 9:24 the prophecy says again, "Seventy weeks are determined upon thy people and upon thy holy city . . . to make an end of sins." The things that happened in Israel during the four hundred and ninety (490) year period brought an end to sins.

How was this possible? The answer is the Cross. The wrath of man manifested against Christ at the Cross-became the means that God used to put away the sins of the elect, and to make an end of sins. On the Cross, the Lord Jesus offered the one sacrifice for sins forever. The Lord did not die in vain. He died in order to purge His people from all their sins.

"Surely the wrath of man shall praise thee: the remainder of wrath shalt thou restrain" (Psalms 76:10).

"For then would they not have ceased to be offered? Because that the worshippers once purged should have had no more conscience of sins" (Heb. 10:2).

"Who being the brightness of his glory, and the express image of his person, and upholding all things by the word of his power, when he had by himself purged our sins, sat down on the right hand of the Majesty on high" (Heb. 1:3).

The third expression in Daniel 9:24 is also instructive. The prophet was told that, "Seventy weeks are determined upon thy people and upon thy holy city . . . to make reconciliation for iniquity." Reconciliation signifies the bringing back together those who were rebels and enemies.

Man has been a rebel against God by nature, and by choice since the fall of Adam. In his heart man has been disloyal, and non-submissive to God. In His justice and righteousness God has had to punish this revolt against Divine authority. Yet the character of God also enjoys displaying grace and mercy.

The only way for grace and mercy to be freely expressed, without compromising justice and righteousness, is for the sin issue to be dealt with. Sin must be punished before there is a basis for reconciliation. Selecting the nation Israel to work through, God the Father decreed a plan of salvation to be expressed in time, with the end result being the making of reconciliation for iniquity. It happened at the Cross. As a result of the death of Christ, those who have redemption through His blood, the forgiveness of sins are reconciled.

> Giving thanks unto the Father, which hath made us meet to be partakers of the inheritance of the saints in light: Who hath delivered us from the power of darkness, and hath translated us into the kingdom of his dear Son: In whom we have redemption through his blood, even the forgiveness of sins: Who is the image of the invisible God, the firstborn of every creature: For

by him were all things created, that are in heaven, and that are in earth, visible and invisible, whether they be thrones, or dominions, or principalities, or powers: all things were created by him, and for him: And he is before all things, and by him all things consist. And he is the head of the body, the church: who is the beginning, the firstborn from the dead; that in all things he might have the preeminence. For it pleased the Father that in him should all fulness dwell; And, having made peace through the blood of his cross, by him to reconcile all things unto himself; by him, I say, whether they be things in earth, or things in heaven. And you, that were sometime alienated and enemies in your mind by wicked works, yet now hath he reconciled In the body of his flesh through death, to present you holy and unblameable and unreproveable in his sight (Col. 1:12–22).

The fourth revelation Daniel was told by the angel Gabriel, is that an everlasting righteousness would be brought in.

"Seventy weeks are determined upon thy people and upon thy holy city . . . to bring in everlasting righteousness" (Dan. 9:24).

Jeremiah had prophesied of this bringing in of righteousness.

"Behold, the days come, saith the Lord, that I will raise unto David a righteous Branch, and a King shall reign and prosper, and shall execute judgment and justice in earth . . .

and this is his name whereby he shall be called, THE LORD OUR RIGHTEOUSNESS" (Jer. 23:6).

Within the four hundred and ninety (490) year time frame it was determined by God, that through the nation Israel, and in the Holy City of Jerusalem, something would happen to bring in everlasting righteousness. Something did happen within the specified time. The Messiah came to Israel and established the kingdom of God in His righteousness, through Jesus Christ.

"But seek ye first the kingdom of God, and his righteousness; and all these things shall be added unto you" (Matt. 6:33).

"For the kingdom of God is not meat and drink; but righteousness, and peace, and joy in the Holy Ghost" (Rom. 14:17).

History records that a work of righteousness was done in Israel on a Cross outside the Holy City. Christ was made unto us righteousness.

"But of him are ye in Christ Jesus, who of God is made unto us wisdom, and righteousness, and sanctification, and redemption" (1 Cor. 1:30).

"For he hath made him to be sin for us, who knew no sin; that we might be made the righteousness of God in him" (2 Cor. 5:21).

The fifth truth the angel told Daniel was that a seal would be placed on the vision and prophecy.

"Seventy years are determined upon thy people and upon thy holy city in order to . . . seal up the vision and prophecy" (Dan. 9:24).

In order to fully appreciate the meaning of these words, it must be kept in mind that the whole vision that Daniel was allowed to see, set forth the goodness, and the severity of God. The goodness of God is manifested in that He was longsuffering with the Jews. The Lord allowed Israel to continue their rebellion against Himself by abusing the prophets, and by killing the Messiah.

The severity of God is manifested in that He was determined to seal up the vision and the prophecy, for "where there is no vision, the people perish" (Prov. 29:18). God can be very severe.

> And he said, Go, and tell this people, Hear ye indeed, but understand not; and see ye indeed, but perceive not. Make the heart of this people fat, and make their ears heavy, and shut their eyes; lest they see with their eyes, and hear with their ears, and understand with their heart, and convert, and be healed (Isa. 6:9–10).

> Stay yourselves, and wonder; cry ye out, and cry: they are drunken, but not with wine; they stagger, but not with strong drink. For the Lord hath poured out upon you the spirit of deep sleep, and hath closed your eyes: the prophets and your rulers, the seers hath he covered (Isa. 29:9–10).

The conclusion of the matter is that the spiritual blindness of national Israel was complete when the Messiah arrived within the designated time frame. Though the

Jewish leaders read the Scriptures daily, they heard not the ancient voices, and so they fulfilled them in condemning Christ.

"Men and brethren, children of the stock of Abraham, and whosoever among you feareth God, to you is the word of this salvation sent" (Acts 13:26).

"Then said Jesus, Father, forgive them; for they know not what they do. And they parted his raiment, and cast lots" (Luke 23:34).

In the New Testament, our Lord applied the prophecy of Isaiah 6:9–10 to the Jews of Israel.

> And he said, Go, and tell this people, Hear ye indeed, but understand not; and see ye indeed, but perceive not. Make the heart of this people fat, and make their ears heavy, and shut their eyes; lest they see with their eyes, and hear with their ears, and understand with their heart, and convert, and be healed (Isa. 6:9–10).

> He answered and said unto them, Because it is given unto you to know the mysteries of the kingdom of heaven, but to them it is not given. For whosoever hath, to him shall be given, and he shall have more abundance: but whosoever hath not, from him shall be taken away even that he hath. Therefore speak I to them in parables: because they seeing see not; and hearing they hear not, neither do they understand" (Matt. 13:11–13).

THE GREATEST PROPHECY EVER FULFILLED

By appealing to the prophet Isaiah, the Lord taught that He Himself was sealing up the visions and the prophecies so that the Jews of His day would have no more light from God because their transgression against God was fulfilled. The ethnic Jew was to know the severity of God. Only the regenerate Jew, only those who had the faith of Abraham, Isaac, and Jacob, only the elect of God would see, and hear and understand.

"But blessed are your eyes, for they see: and your ears, for they hear" (Matt. 13:16).

> But though he had done so many miracles before them, yet they believed not on him: That the saying of Esaias the prophet might be fulfilled, which he spake, Lord, who hath believed our report? And to whom hath the arm of the Lord been revealed? Therefore they could not believe, because that Esaias said again, He hath blinded their eyes, and hardened their heart; that they should not see with their eyes, nor understand with their heart, and be converted, and I should heal them. These things said Esaias, when he saw his glory, and spake of him (John 12:37–41).

> And some believed the things which were spoken, and some believed not. And when they agreed not among themselves, they departed, after that Paul had spoken one word, Well spake the Holy Ghost by Esaias the prophet unto our fathers, Saying, Go unto this people, and say, Hearing ye shall hear,

and shall not understand; and seeing ye shall see, and not perceive: For the heart of this people is waxed gross, and their ears are dull of hearing, and their eyes have they closed; lest they should see with their eyes, and hear with their ears, and understand with their heart, and should be converted, and I should heal them (Acts 28:24–27).

Behold therefore the goodness and severity of God: on them which fell, severity; but toward thee, goodness, if thou continue in his goodness: otherwise thou also shalt be cut off (Rom. 11:22).

Returning to Daniel 9:24, there is a sixth prophetic event the angel shared with the prophet.

Seventy weeks are determined upon thy people and upon thy holy city . . . to anoint the Most High.

The Most High is the Lord Jesus Christ. Of Himself the Lord said,

> The Spirit of the Lord is upon me, because He hath anointed me to preach the gospel to the poor; He hath sent me to heal the broken hearted, to preach deliverance to the captives, and recovering of sight to the blind, to set at liberty them that are bruised, to preach the acceptable year of the Lord (Luke 4:18–19).

For three and one half (3½) years the Lord Jesus did all of this before He was "cut off for His people" (Dan. 9:26).

All four Gospels describe in detail, "How God anointed Jesus of Nazareth with the Holy Spirit and with power: who went about doing good, and healing all that were oppressed of the devil; for God was with Him" (Acts 10:38).

The ultimate anointing of the Most Holy person of Christ came with His resurrection, as Hebrews 1:9 explains. He was anointed with the oil of gladness above His fellows. Paul declares that,

> God hath highly exalted Him, and given Him a name which is above every name: that at the name of Jesus every knee should bow, of things in heaven, and things in earth, and things under the earth; and that every tongue should confess that Jesus Christ is Lord to the glory of God the Father (Phil. 2:9–11).

In Daniel 9:25 the certainty of all the prophetic utterances being fulfilled is reinforced by further details being given concerning the time frame. Daniel is instructed to know certain truths. "From the going forth of the commandment to restore and to build Jerusalem unto the Messiah the Prince shall be seven weeks, and three score and two weeks: the street shall be built again, and the wall, even in troublous times" (Dan. 9:25).

Within the four hundred and eighty three (483) years [7 weeks of 7 years = 49 years + 62 weeks of 7 years = 434 years or 49 + 434 = 483 years] from the issuing of the royal decree to restore and to rebuild Jerusalem, the Messiah did appear.

When the Messiah came there were souls who recognized Him because He was expected.

"He first findeth his own brother Simon, and saith unto him, We have found the Messias, which is, being interpreted, the Christ" (John 1:41).

> And, behold, there was a man in Jerusalem, whose name was Simeon; and the same man was just and devout, waiting for the consolation of Israel: and the Holy Ghost was upon him. And it was revealed unto him by the Holy Ghost, that he should not see death, before he had seen the Lord's Christ. And he came by the Spirit into the temple: and when the parents brought in the child Jesus, to do for him after the custom of the law, Then took he him up in his arms, and blessed God, and said, Lord, now lettest thou thy servant depart in peace, according to thy word: For mine eyes have seen thy salvation, Which thou hast prepared before the face of all people; A light to lighten the Gentiles, and the glory of thy people Israel. And Joseph and his mother marvelled at those things which were spoken of him. And Simeon blessed them, and said unto Mary his mother, Behold, this child is set for the fall and rising again of many in Israel; and for a sign which shall be spoken against; (Yea, a sword shall pierce through thy own soul also,) that

the thoughts of many hearts may be revealed (Luke 2:25–35).

The heart of Daniel must have shuddered at the next statement of the holy angel. It was revealed that the promised Messiah would die. ". . . after threescore and two weeks [i.e. after the 483 years] shall Messiah be cut off, but not for Himself" (Dan. 9:26).

The time period is plain. Within the first seven weeks, or forty-nine (49) years Jerusalem was to be rebuilt, following the Babylonian Captivity. Then, after four hundred and thirty four (434) more years the Messiah was to appear. Next would come the final one week of seven (7) years.

Two questions are raised.

First, did the final, seventieth (70th) week, follow the sixty ninth week?

Second, at what point in the Messiah's ministry did the prophecy occur which would mark the *beginning* of the final week?

The key to understanding the answer is in the name "Messiah." After four hundred and eighty three (483) years, Messiah was to appear. After four hundred and eighty three (483) years Messiah did appear to Israel at the river Jordan in the person of Jesus Christ. Peter bore witness to this fact when he said that God anointed Jesus of Nazareth with the Holy Spirit and with power.

"How God anointed Jesus of Nazareth with the Holy Ghost and with power: who went about doing good, and healing all that were oppressed of the devil; for God was with him" (Acts 10:38).

The baptism of Jesus marked precisely when the seventieth (70th) week began.

In this final seven (7) year period of one prophetic week the six predicted features of Daniel 9:24 came to fulfillment as well as the features of Daniel 9:27, whereby the Messiah caused "the sacrifice and the oblation to cease."

". . . He [the Messiah] shall confirm the covenant with many for one week: and in the midst of the week He shall cause the sacrifice and the oblation to cease . . ." (Dan. 9:27).

The pronoun reference "He" in Daniel 9:27 can only refer to the Messiah of Daniel 9:26, and no one else. It was the Messiah who was prophesied to confirm the covenant with many for one week.

Here is one of the most alarming facts in all of church history. A traditional Messianic passage was reinterpreted in the nineteenth century to refer to an anti-Christ. Dear Lord, how did that happen!

The word for confirm, in Daniel 9:27 means "to ratify." Since it is not possible to confirm, or ratify something unless it is in existence, the covenant that the Messiah ratified must have been in existence. Theologians refer to this existing covenant as the Covenant of Works, which was first made with Adam in the Garden of Eden.

"And the Lord God commanded the man, saying, Of every tree of the garden thou mayest freely eat: But of the tree of the knowledge of good and evil, thou shalt not eat of it: for in the day that thou eatest thereof thou shalt surely die" (Gen. 2:16–17).

The provisions of the Covenant were that obedience brought life, and disobedience brought judgment, and death. The First Adam failed to keep the provision of obedience, thereby breaking the Covenant of Works. The Last Adam [the Messiah] did not fail to be obedient, but fulfilled all the provisions of the Covenant of Works. He was perfect. The Messiah kept all of the Law of Moses, and then He did more. The Messiah instituted a New Covenant of Grace, based upon His substitutionary death at Calvary.

The New Covenant is an everlasting covenant. It was instituted during the last week of Daniel's prophetic vision, but is destined to endure for eternity. This New Covenant of Grace is explained in detail in Hebrews 8 and 9. In Hebrews 8:8–13 and 10:15–17 the Holy Author of scripture declares that the New Covenant of Matthew 26:28 is the fulfillment of the promise of Jeremiah 31:31–34.

The New Covenant Fulfills the Promises of Jeremiah the Prophet

> For finding fault with them, he saith, Behold, the days come, saith the Lord, when I will make a new covenant with the house of Israel and with the house of Judah: Not according to the covenant that I made with their fathers in the day when I took them by the hand to lead them out of the land of Egypt; because they continued not in my

covenant, and I regarded them not, saith the Lord. For this is the covenant that I will make with the house of Israel after those days, saith the Lord; I will put my laws into their mind, and write them in their hearts: and I will be to them a God, and they shall be to me a people: And they shall not teach every man his neighbour, and every man his brother, saying, Know the Lord: for all shall know me, from the least to the greatest. For I will be merciful to their unrighteousness, and their sins and their iniquities will I remember no more. In that he saith, A new covenant, he hath made the first old. Now that which decayeth and waxeth old is ready to vanish away (Heb. 8:8–13).

Whereof the Holy Ghost also is a witness to us: for after that he had said before, This is the covenant that I will make with them after those days, saith the Lord, I will put my laws into their hearts, and in their minds will I write them; And their sins and iniquities will I remember no more (Heb. 10:15–17).

The New Covenant of Grace, confirmed by the Messiah, is said to be made with "many" according to Daniel 9:27. Not all people shall be saved, but many will be. The New Testament agrees. Matthew 1:21 declares that the Messiah was to, Save His people from their sins. In Matthew 26:28 Jesus said, "This is my blood of the New Covenant shed for many for the remissions of sins."

"He shall see of the travail of his soul, and shall be satisfied: by his knowledge shall my righteous servant justify many; for he shall bear their iniquities" (Isa. 53:11).

"And many of the children of Israel shall he turn to the Lord their God" (Luke 1:16).

"And Simeon blessed them, and said unto Mary his mother, Behold, this child is set for the fall and rising again of many in Israel; and for a sign which shall be spoken against" (Luke 2:34).

"Even as the Son of man came not to be ministered unto, but to minister, and to give his life a ransom for many" (Matt. 20:28).

"For as by one man's disobedience many were made sinners, so by the obedience of one shall many be made righteous" (Rom. 5:19).

While "confirming the covenant" in fulfillment of Daniel 9:27, the Messiah was able to cause the sacrifice and the oblation to cease. With these words the prophecy was made that the Messiah would make an end to all the Old Testament sacrifices, if not in literal practice, at least as to their necessity.

Hebrews 8—10 sets forth in great detail, and with great emphasis the abolishing of the demands of the Law of Moses with all the sacrifices and ritual. For the Christian community the sacrifices of bulls and goats have ceased. Hebrews 10:9 is the fulfillment of Daniel 9:27. The reality of the death of Christ dispels the shadows forever.

And he shall confirm the covenant with many for one week: and in the midst of the week he shall cause the sacrifice and the oblation to cease, and for the overspreading of abominations he shall make it desolate, even until the consummation, and that determined shall be poured upon the desolate (Dan. 9:27).

Then said he, Lo, I come to do thy will, O God. He taketh away the first, that he may establish the second (Heb. 10:9).

The final important phrase of Daniel 9:27 is that which says the work of the Messiah would be such that the way would be paved . . . "for the overspreading of abominations; he shall make it desolate, even until consummation, and that determined shall be poured upon the desolate."

The Revised Standard Version makes this passage a little easier to understand: "and upon the wing of abominations shall come one who makes desolate, until the decreed end is poured out on the desolate."

The desolate was Israel, who had killed the prophets of God. Israel had also rejected the Messiah. Israel had refused to repent. Israel had crucified the Lord of Glory. God therefore decreed that Israel would be made desolate in fulfillment of Daniel's prophecy, and it was.

In all of its essential parts, the prophecy given to Daniel was fulfilled.

There is only one other factor to consider, and that is the reference by the Lord to "the abomination of desolation spoken of by Daniel the prophet standing in the Holy Place" (Matt. 24:15).

As the Lord was fulfilling the prophecy of Daniel, He appealed to the prophet's previous prediction concerning Antiochus Epiphanes IV who was the ruler of Syria from 175–164 B.C.

Antiochus was the "little horn" of Daniel 8:9.

"And out of one of them came forth a little horn, which waxed exceeding great, toward the south, and toward the east, and toward the pleasant land" (Dan. 8:9).

In a vain attempt to influence the Jews with Greek culture, Antiochus performed an abomination of desolation when he offered to Zeus a pig on the altar of the Holy Temple in Jerusalem, thereby desecrating the holy altar.

With that historical allusion in mind, Jesus, in Matthew 24:15 tells the Jews that the same type of thing will happen again in their generation. The Lord had in mind the destruction of the Temple by the Romans. "When ye therefore shall see the abomination of desolation, spoken of by Daniel the prophet, stand in the holy place, (whoso readeth, let him understand)" (Matt. 24:15).

The desecration and destruction of the Holy Temple would have happened soon after the death of Christ except for one fact. While He was on the Cross-Jesus prayed for the people, and God delayed the execution of His judgment until A.D. 70.

In A.D. 70, Israel was made even more desolate than in 167 B.C. under the reign of Antiochus Epiphanes, for there did come one upon the wings of abominations, in the person of the Roman general Titus.

In A.D. 70 Rome was weary of the Jewish revolts. For three and one half (3½) years Rome laid seize to Jerusalem, and finally conquered the city completely. The Holy Temple was destroyed and the prophecy of Christ in Matthew 24:15, using a previous typology provided by Daniel in the form of Antiochus, was finally fulfilled.

Bibliography

Boettner, Loraine. *The Millennium*: Phillipsburg: Presbyterian and Reformed, 1957.

de Botton, Alain. *The Consolations of Philosophy*. London: Penguin Books, 2000.

Edersheim, Alfred. *The Life and Times of Jesus the Messiah*. Peabody: Hendrickson Publishers, 1993,

Gentry, Kenneth L. *Before Jerusalem Fell*. Tyler: Institute for Christian Economics, 1989.

Gill, John. *An Exposition of the New Testament*. London: Mathews and Leigh, 1809.

Henry, Matthew. *Commentary on the Whole Bible*. Peabody: Hendrickson Publishers, 1991.

Josephus, *The Complete Works of Flavius Josephus*. Green Forest: Master Books, 2008.

LeHaye, Tim and Jenkins, Jerry B. *Left Behind*. Carol Stream: Tyndale House Publishers; Reprint edition (March 16, 2011) 496.

Kimball, William R. *The Great Tribulation*. Phillipsburg: Presbyterian and Reformed, 1983.

Sawyer, James M. *The Survivor's Guide to Theology*. Grand Rapids: Zondervan, 2006.

Schaff, Philip. *History of the Christian Church*. Vol. 1. Grand Rapids: WM. B. Eerdmans, 1966.

Swete, Henry B. *Commentary on Revelation*. Grand Rapids: Kregel, 1906.

www.ingramcontent.com/pod-product-compliance
Lightning Source LLC
Chambersburg PA
CBHW061445040426
42450CB00007B/1230